SECRETS OF THE STOICS

How to Live an Undefeatable Life

JASON HEMLOCK

SECRETS OF THE STOICS:
How to Live an Undefeatable Life
by Jason Hemlock

© Copyright 2021 by Jason Hemlock

All Rights Reserved.

Disclaimer: This book is designed to provide accurate and authoritative information regarding the subject matter covered. By its sale, neither the publisher nor the author is engaged in rendering psychological or other professional services. If expert assistance or counselling is needed, the services of a competent professional should be sought.

ISBN: 979-8781631506

CONTENTS

FOREWORD

I f you are looking to build off the concepts shared in this book, I encourage you to check out my journaling book, *Practicing Stoicism: A Daily Journal with Meditation Practices, Self-Reflections and Ancient Wisdom from Marcus Aurelius*. There you will find daily inspirational quotes from Marcus Aurelius, morning journaling prompts to help you develop a Stoic attitude, daily exercises to bring Stoic practices to life and evening journaling prompts so you can track the difference Stoicism is making in your life. The daily exercises presented in the journal are based off what you learned in this book so reading it at the same time and/or after will help you get even more out of this one.

If you want to continue reading about Stoicism, please check out my other book, *Stoicism: How to Use Stoic Philosophy to Find Inner Peace and Happiness*. This book will provide you with even more tools and practices to assist you on your Stoic journey.

Also, as a way of saying thank you for purchasing this book, I'm offering a three-page Stoicism cheat sheet for free. To claim it, sign up for my email list where you will receive updates and future content from me. The cheat sheet includes quotes from some of my favorite Stoics and a short summary of the principles that were discussed in this book, which you can use for future reference.

You can sign up here: bouchardpublishing.com/stoicism

INTRODUCTION

"Throw out your conceited opinions, for it is impossible for a person to begin to learn what he thinks he already knows."

—Epictetus

t seems like no matter how advanced our society becomes, we still do not seem to be able to find simple solutions to life's most fundamental problems. Our iPhone might give us the internet in the palm of our hand, but it can't heal the pain of a broken heart. We might be able to travel the world in a matter of days rather than months, but we still grieve the loss of those we love. The 2020 pandemic highlighted that society is still divided, stressful, and difficult to navigate.

While we want to look forward to building a brighter future, many people are finding that they can find help and support by turning to the past. More specifically, the ancient past, when Greek and Roman philosophers considered the exact same questions and problems which trouble us today – and came up with effective solutions.

As the centuries passed and the powerful Greek and Roman empires crumbled, much of that ancient wisdom was forgotten about or ignored. Fortunately, the ancients lived in a highly literate society, which means that we still have access to the original texts containing the powerful principles of their philosophies to discover that they believed in living a good life in which you live up to your potential and take advantage of every single opportunity that comes your way.

One of those philosophies was Stoicism, a Hellenistic philosophy that has become popular again over the past twenty years or so. It provides followers with exercises, mindsets, and attitudes that empower adherents to live a good life. There is a strong emphasis on self-discipline and personal improvement, which, if followed on a daily basis, allows the individual to feel that they have truly reached their potential.

This isn't just theory. Stoicism has become popular with leaders, top businesspeople, entrepreneurs, world class musicians, artists, and actors. These include:

- Arnold Schwarzenegger, who has reached the top of every field he's turned his hand to – he was a holder of the Mr. Olympia title, going on to become an A-list Hollywood celebrity before turning to politics, where he became Governor of California, the highest political office someone can hold who was not born in the United States.
- Bill Clinton, former American president, and Wen Jiabao, former Chinese Prime Minister, both of whom have read Marcus Aurelius' *Meditations* multiple times.
- Thomas Jefferson, one of the Founding Fathers of America, who died leaving a copy of Seneca's essays by his bedside.
- George Washington, the first President of the United States, who started learning about Stoicism as a teenager and was reported to have used the philosophy as a guide to his leadership style.
- Many leading coaches use Stoicism to inspire their teams, such as Joe Maddon, Chicago Cubs manager, and Seattle Seahawks head coach Pete Carrol. Meanwhile, the New England Patriots have won five Super Bowls and apparently incorporate Stoic thinking into their training practices.

- In *East of Eden,* Nobel Prize winning author John Steinbeck makes reference to *Meditations.* He is not the only writer to have used Stoicism in his work; Ralph Waldo Emerson, an essayist, philosopher, and poet, also used the philosophy for inspiration.
- Another author, Tim Ferriss (*The Four Hour Work Week*), who also hosts a podcast and is an angel investor, has often spoken about how valuable he finds Stoicism. He has even published an audiobook of Seneca's letters so others can discover how useful Stoicism can be.
- Admiral James Stockdale was a prisoner of war in Vietnam. During his seven-year imprisonment, his Stoic approach was what enabled him to survive.
- Multi-platinum selling Grammy winner T-Pain released an album entitled *Stoicville* and the *Stoic* mixtape. Another Grammy Award winner, rapper Lupe Fiasco, quotes Marcus Aurelius in his lyrics. Further, he's tweeted to his fans that if they want to understand him better, they should read *Meditations.*
- Actress, singer, and author Anna Kendrick has described *Meditations* as being 'comforting.' Fellow actor Tom Hiddleston is a big fan of Seneca's *On the Shortness of Life.*

If all these successful people can find inspiration, support, and help from the ancient Stoics, it is no wonder that many others are turning to Stoicism to achieve their goals and improve their wellbeing.

At its core, Stoicism has one basic tenet: it is up to you, the individual, to take control and responsibility for all of your thoughts and behaviors. If you can do this, you are well on the way to personal fulfilment. Stoicism is suitable for anyone, regardless of your current situation, health status, religion, talents, career, relationship status, and so on. Whatever you want to do with your life, Stoicism will help you get to where you want to go. After all, it has worked for U.S. Presidents and Grammy winners!

As if that wasn't enough, when you live a Stoic life, Stoicism can do more than simply help you be a better person. It has the potential to change the world, improving things not just for you but for everyone.

What is Stoicism?

Sometime around 304 BC, a successful, rich merchant, Zeno of Citium, was traveling across seas when he was shipwrecked. He lost almost everything, but as he found his way to Athens, he encountered Crates of Thebes, a famous Cynic who introduced him to philosophy. This meeting was to change his life – and the face of philosophy. Within a few short years, Zeno became the father of Stoic philosophy. He later quipped, "I made a prosperous voyage when I suffered shipwreck."

Zeno taught philosophy at the 'Stoa Poikile' (painted porch), which is what gave rise to the name Stoicism. The Stoa Poikile was a colonnade situated by the Agora in Athens. Even without the philosophical thoughts behind Stoicism, the fact that Zeno chose such a public place sent a very clear signal that what he was doing was innovative, as few philosophers of the time were willing to teach in public places.

Over time, other talented philosophers built upon the foundation Zeno had laid until the movement was fully formed. Stoicism found popularity throughout the Roman and Greek Empires until the 3rd century AD, when it fell out of favor and gradually died down as Christianity became the state religion of Rome. However, it enjoyed sporadic resurgences, especially during the Renaissance and, of course, in modern times.

One of the most famous – and most quoted – ancient followers of Stoicism was Emperor Marcus Aurelius. He made a point of journaling every day and, while most of his letters and works have been lost over the years, his *Meditations* is considered to be a seminal text that should be read by anyone wishing to follow a Stoic way of life.

One of the basic principles of Stoicism is that true happiness is found by accepting each moment as it comes and understanding that it is what it is without judgment. This attitude is similar to that found in modern mindfulness, another popular modern movement.

Stoicism teaches the individual to rise above base motivations, such a fear or hedonism, but instead look to understand the world around them, live in harmony with others, and discover their place in nature to fulfil their purpose. According to Stoicism, goals such as greater wealth or improved health do not have any inherent goodness or bad, but instead are opportunities to allow the individual to live a virtuous life. This notion of virtuousness was very important to the Stoics and is what gave rise to the modern word 'stoic,' as the ancient Stoics were known to deprive themselves of luxuries and treats as part of their philosophy. As a result, according to the dictionary, someone who is stoic is someone who is able to cope with hard times without complaining. While it is certainly true that following a Stoic philosophy will enable you to do this, this is just one of the many benefits.

As Marcus Aurelius said, "If it is endurable, then endure it. Stop complaining." After all, complaining rarely solves a problem and only serves to make you feel worse, so it is better to take a Stoic approach and accept things as they are rather than moaning that they are not the way you want them to be.

This approach to life means that someone who follows a Stoic philosophy develops the mental resilience to cope with difficult situations that may make someone else crumble under the stress. However, this doesn't mean that Stoics are trying to ignore their emotions or inure themselves to pain; rather, their aim is to free themselves from letting their emotions run their life through the use of logic and reason. Ultimately, Stoicism is a lifelong process aimed at furthering one's levels of self-control, self-awareness, and self-discipline.

At its heart, Stoicism is a philosophy that needs to be put into practice. It is not enough to study it or memorize quotes. The only way to truly be a Stoic is to see those beliefs and attitudes in reality through your behavior.

Stoicism draws inspiration from nature. If you follow the tides of life, it is natural to experience bad times after the good in a cycle that features ups and downs as a matter of course. The more you can work with these tides, the better and more fulfilling your life will be.

Four reasons why you should follow Stoicism

Given how many high achievers subscribe to a Stoic way of life, it should be clear that Stoicism genuinely changes lives for the better, enabling individuals to achieve their potential and feel happy and content at the same time. But just in case you needed a few more reasons to start your Stoic journey, here are four specific ones, which should convince you that the time has come to start following Stoicism.

Stoicism supports you through hardship

Stoicism evolved during a time of great turbulence and upheaval. It wasn't that long after Alexander the Great had conquered the world that he died prematurely in his early thirties, likely of typhoid fever. His death naturally had major consequences for his Empire, the future of which was questionable.

With all this uncertainty, Stoicism provided its followers a framework that enabled them to find security in unpredictable times, helping them to stay grounded regardless of what happened next. Whereas religion ultimately encouraged its believers to put their trust and faith in rewards that came after death, Stoicism kept its focus firmly on finding contentment in the now.

Ever heard the saying, 'Life is what happens when you're busy making plans'? Even when you think you know what's going to happen, life has a funny way of throwing you a curveball. Stoicism teaches us not to rely on anything that can change. Your bank balance goes up and down all the time. Friendships and relationships can end for the most spurious of reasons. The only constant throughout all of this is you. Every single second, we are making a choice about how we react to what is happening around us. When it comes down to it, the *only* thing we have control over is ourselves.

It is only natural to react negatively when something happens that hurts us, but under a Stoic philosophy, you should aim to rise above whatever is going on around you and find positivity in your life, regardless of whether life is easy or not. Although this peace of mind can be difficult to maintain when you first begin practising Stoicism, once you've managed to cultivate control over your mind, you free yourself from being ruled by emotion, giving you even more control over the rest of your life. While you still might feel upset when faced with a challenge, a Stoic can put negative emotions into perspective and not allow them to become a problem.

These days, we are facing a similar level of political upheaval to that dealt with by the ancient Stoics. It would be a natural step to use Stoicism to help you deal with everything that is going on right now.

As Epictetus said, "It isn't the things themselves that disturb people, but the judgements that they form about them."

Stoicism makes you more tolerant and accepting of others

Ancient Graeco-Roman society was highly diverse, but there were strong divides along lines of nationality, religion, and social status.

This made Stoicism revolutionary by maybe being the first Western philosophy to teach that all men are equal, regardless of whether they are a slave or emperor, summed up by Epictetus when he wrote that we are all "a member of the great city of gods and men."

Because Stoicism teaches that true happiness can only be found inside ourselves rather than through any external event, taken to its logical conclusion, social divides become nonsensical and unnecessary. While Stoicism might not have been enough to make the ancient Greeks and Romans free their slaves, the Stoics taught that we all live under the same sky. We all bleed when we are cut. We all need the same basics: food, shelter, love. As such, we all deserve respect, regardless of our background.

Bringing this attitude into a modern context, Stoicism helps us to appreciate and accept the glorious spectrum of the human experience, seeing no race, religion, culture, or creed as being superior or inferior to any other.

You can be a Stoic regardless of your religious background

If you follow a religion, you might be concerned about whether Stoicism is compatible with your faith. However, when you examine the philosophy, you'll see some striking similarities between Stoic tenets and the main religions.

In common with the prevailing faiths of the time, Stoicism teaches that:

- There is a single, unifying God with multiple facets.
- You should always follow your conscience and live a moral, ethical life.
- You should rise above your negative impulses and choose the high road.

Christianity was a new religion at the time when Stoicism developed and many Stoic notions found their way into the faith, so much so that these days we are more likely to associate those concepts with religion rather than philosophy. Stoicism had a major influence on Roman society for centuries, so it was only natural that Christianity would adopt many of these existing ideas. Indeed, many early Christian leaders had been proponents of Stoicism before they joined the Church, so they naturally brought their existing attitudes with them and adapted them to a Christian way of thinking.

In fact, it is not an exaggeration to say that for the early Church, religious thought was tantamount to Stoic thought.

As Christianity developed further and grew to become a school of thought in its own right, church leaders moved away from Stoicism in favor of promoting their own religion. However, while we can trace some Christian practices back to pagan customs, we can also see Stoic philosophy in some of the most fundamental Christian concepts, making it perfectly compatible with the religion.

Stoicism makes leaders

If you want to be a leader in any shape or form, Stoicism provides you with the foundation you need to be an effective, successful leader, one who inspires others to follow. It gives you the ability to push through failures and setbacks and keeps you grounded so your ego doesn't get out of control when things are going well.

By default, any leader has an impact on the world around them. This can give rise to the temptation to attempt to control events, but under Stoicism, you learn to control yourself first, which eliminates any desire to control others. No matter how much you may want it to be different, the only thing you have control over is yourself. If you kid yourself that it can be otherwise, you're only setting yourself up for disappointment. But if you are able to master yourself, allowing you to identify the best course of action in any situation, you'll discover that anything else is a gift.

While change is the only constant in life, a leader is particularly vulnerable to changing circumstances because they are the ones ultimately responsible when things go wrong. A Stoic mindset can help you maintain your calm in the most difficult of situations, allowing you to keep a clear head and prioritize where your attention should be going and identify what you can delegate or leave until later.

While Barack Obama may not be a Stoic in the technical sense, there are many instances in which he could be said to be following Stoic principles. For example, he has said that while he was President, he did his best to reduce the number of decisions he had to make on any given day. As a result, he let other people choose what he was going to eat or wear. When he had so many important decisions to make all the time, his attitude was that "you can't be going through the day distracted by trivia." This attitude of only focusing on what's important is pure Stoicism.

The Stoics understood that failure was a natural part of life that comes to us all, and this is perfectly fine. They were fully aware that the human experience ran the entire gamut of emotions, positive and negative, so they found a way of dealing with them, which made it easier to navigate life's rocky roads. After all, it is easy to be philosophical during the good times. It's when things get hard that it is difficult to maintain that same attitude. Stoicism makes it simple for you to establish healthy mental attitudes and habits, which will help you to deal with anything that happens.

In this book, you will learn more about famous ancient Stoics and how their philosophy helped them in their lives. We will look closely at the principles that made them so successful and discuss how they can be applied in a modern context to improve your life. You will also receive practical exercises that you can start working with immediately, so you can quickly see the positive impact of Stoicism on your life.

As Seneca puts it, "While we wait for life, life passes."

Don't let your life pass you by. Learn the secrets of the Stoics and see the positive impact they can have on your wellbeing today.

PART ONE:

EPICTETUS

THE LIFE OF EPICTETUS

If you want to improve, be content to be thought
foolish and stupid.

—Epictetus

Epictetus was born sometime around 50AD, probably in Hierapolis, Phrygia. His original name is unknown; 'Epictetus' comes from a Greek word meaning 'gained' or 'acquired' and was presumably given to him when he was enslaved as a child. He spent his youth in Rome where his wealthy freedman master, Epaphroditos, was a secretary to the Emperor Nero.

Epictetus discovered a love for philosophy while he was still young, and his owner gave him permission to study Stoic philosophy under the guidance of Musonius Rufus. While there is no doubt that these teachings shaped how Epictetus dealt with the realities of being a slave, his education also meant that his social status grew.

We do not know when or how Epictetus became disabled, another difficulty Stoicism helped him with. Origen claimed that this was as a consequence of his master breaking his leg, which failed to heal properly. However, according to Simplicius, Epictetus had been disabled since he was a child.

After Nero died in 68AD, Epictetus was freed and he started to teach philosophy in Rome. When Emperor Domitian banished all philosophers from Rome, Epictetus moved to Nicopolis in Epirus,

Greece, sometime around 93AD. It was here that his most famous pupil, Arrian, came to learn from him, roughly fifteen years later, and is said to have written his *Discourses* based on notes he'd taken during lectures. According to Arrian, Epictetus was a charismatic lecturer who could "induce his listener to feel just what Epictetus wanted him to feel." Many important, prominent people from the time consulted with him, such as the Emperor Hadrian, who may even have been to see him speak at his school in Nicopolis.

True to his Stoic beliefs, Epictetus lived a simple life, having very little in the way of possessions. He lived alone for much of his life, becoming a parent late in adulthood when he adopted a friend's child who was going to be left to die. Epictetus raised him with the support of a woman, although it is unknown whether they were a married couple.

The exact date of Epictetus' death is unknown, but it is believed to be sometime around 135AD.

Epictetus' philosophy

Although there are no surviving writings from Epictetus himself, Arrian transcribed much of his philosophy, gathering them together in various works, the most important of which is *The Discourses,* a series of eight books (four of which have survived to modern times). In the preface, which is addressed to Lucius Gellius, Arrian wrote, "Whatever I heard [Epictetus] say I used to write down, word for word, as best I could, endeavouring to preserve it as a memorial, for my own future use, of his way of thinking and the frankness of his speech."

Epictetus held that the founding principle of any philosophical practice is self-knowledge and that anyone wanting to elevate their understandings should first pay attention to their own ignorance and gullibility.

While applying logic to theoretical situations was helpful, practical application and demands were more important.

First, and most important, is the application of any given philosophical doctrine, such as the importance of not stealing. Next comes an examination of reasons as to why someone should not steal. Finally, a philosopher would then examine those reasons to determine their validity.

Both *Discourses* and another work by Epictetus, the *Enchiridion,* start by defining the difference between what is within someone's power (*prohairetic* things) and that which is not (*aprohairetic* things). Once we start examining this point, we soon discover that the only things that are in anyone's power are their opinions, urges, wants, loves, and hates. Anything else is outside your control. It is when you forget this that you make your biggest mistakes, discover the greatest misery, and fall into the so-called slavery of the soul. As such, the good that Stoics hold to be the highest goal can only be found by looking within yourself.

As Epictetus stated, "Things in our control are opinion, pursuit, desire, aversion, and, in a word, whatever are our own actions. Things not in our control are body, property, reputation, command, and, in one word, whatever are not our own actions." Further, "Freedom is the only worthy goal in life. It is won by disregarding things that lie beyond our control."

Given this, if you are able to fully embrace his philosophy, it would mean that when you lose something, whether it be an object, relationship, job, and so on, this would not bother you because it was never yours in the first place, being something outside of your power. Instead, you get to find good or evil in the choices you make, which will empower you to find peace of mind, whatever happens.

Another important concept, according to Epictetus, is that we are all connected with the rest of the world and the natural order of the universe is one of harmony. As such, if someone is wise, they will follow not just what is best and right for them but also what is best and right for the world at large. We should all aim to meet our obligations to those around us – children, family, citizens – and do so in a manner that supports the highest good.

According to Epictetus, we should all be willing to make the ultimate sacrifice for those around us if need be. A truly good person, if they knew what was coming, would willingly and happily bring about their own illness, maiming, death even, secure in the knowledge that this was all part of the natural order of the universe. We all have a specific role to play according to our nature and when we fulfil our purpose, we have done everything we need. By learning more about ourselves and following our true nature, we may even uncover our purpose and destiny, leading to greater personal fulfilment. As a Stoic, it does not matter what life throws at us, we are able to bear it without complaint; for those who are not yet ready to embrace this approach, we should forgive them and offer them compassion because they are still ignorant.

After all, the only things that can make us unhappy are our personal opinions and principles, and because these are in our control, we can actively choose those which make us happy. We can rise above our petty desires to experience true freedom, just as Epictetus did.

THE SECRET TO ENJOYING A SIMPLE LIFE

Wealth consists not in having great possessions,
but in having few wants.
—Epictetus

A t the moment, minimalism is very popular. There are number of reasons why people may want to simplify their life – they may want to save money or time; reduce stress or anxiety; be more environmentally conscious; choose to spend their money on experiences rather than things; or simply have friends, parents, or a spouse who are minimalist.

However, there are also those who are merely virtue signaling, being minimalist as a fashion choice or to fit in. They may even try to outdo others in how minimalist they are, boasting about their latest attempts at simplifying their life rather than quietly getting on with it.

This is where you need to be very honest with yourself about your motivations. If you truly want to live a simple life, you need to take a Stoic approach. As Seneca puts it, "We should not believe the lack of silver and gold to be proof of the simple life." Possessions – or the lack thereof – do not define a simple life. You could be a multimillionaire, traveling the world on a private jet and enjoying perfect inner harmony, while someone with very little money and belongings could be filled with resentment. Turning your back on consumerism but choosing to use this as an opportunity to show off how morally superior you are to everyone isn't exactly in the spirit of Stoicism. Likewise, if you're always focusing on how much money you can save by not buying things, keeping track of every single nickel and dime to the point where you become obsessed with all the dollars you're not spending, you're hardly enjoying peace of mind.

A true simple life is, well, simple. Grateful. Filled with appreciation for whatever you have, regardless of the size of your bank balance, or the quality of the food you eat.

The secret to enjoying a simple life is that it's not about a lack of money or possessions, but rather a lack of want and need, a lack of envy, a lack of stress, a lack of insecurity, and a lack of resentment.

This is true wealth. Minimalism is just one tool to help you focus on what's truly important in life. And if you look into what minimalism is truly about, it doesn't place any limits on what you can own or choose to buy; it merely means that you become more aware of what you have and whether you really need it and if it brings genuine happiness to you. If you want an expensive car, you can have one. If you want to buy a house, you can. If you want the latest iPhone, you can treat yourself. Just be aware of your motives and reasonings. Being minimalist means being intentional in your choices and living with less, mainly essential items. It involves overcoming the urge to buy, buy, buy and keep up with the Joneses. It allows you to free yourself from the expectations of society and other people so you can be more aware and make choices that are right for you.

There are many lessons you can learn if you choose to be more minimalist and live like Epictetus.

1. **Material possessions are outside of your control.**

   As Epictetus put it, "Material things are indifferent, but how we handle them is not indifferent." After all, our possessions can be destroyed, lost, or stolen. They are neither good nor bad but rather indifferent because they are outside of our control. This does not mean that you can't choose to have those things that bring you pleasure – it is preferable to be wealthy than live in poverty – but no importance should be placed on them because they are not completely within your control. Therefore, don't place too much meaning on anything you own or become too attached. You never know what might happen. If you start to worry about losing what you have, you automatically lose your happiness and freedom. Nothing really belongs to any of us, so don't give your belongings any importance.

2. **The only thing you can control are your thoughts.**

   Think about your home for a moment. Whether you own or rent it, is it ever really truly yours? Will it be demolished when you die? Did people live in it before you did? Will they live there after your gone? No matter how much you might believe something is yours, realistically we're only ever borrowing it for an indeterminate amount of time.

   There is but one thing you own: your mind. Of course, you can enjoy your possessions while you have them, but you should always remember that they are never really yours. Eventually they'll be gone from your life.

3. **Being minimalist in your words and deeds will make you a better communicator.**

Epictetus said, "Let silence be your goal for the most part; say only what is necessary and be brief about it. On the rare occasions when you're called upon to speak, then speak, but never about banalities like gladiators, horses, sports, food and drink – common-place stuff. Above all don't gossip about people, praising, blaming or comparing them."

Most of us don't listen when we're having a conversation. Instead, we're sitting there, patiently (or not!) waiting our turn to share the brilliant thought we had as soon as the other person started speaking.

According to the Stoics, however, much of what we say is pointless. Instead, before saying or doing anything, ask yourself, is this really necessary? The chances are, it won't be. Taking this attitude will force you to pay more attention to what the other person is saying so you truly listen. Key to communication is understanding what someone else is saying, so if you put the focus on the other person rather than yourself, you'll be amazed at how much better your powers of communication become.

4. **You really don't need very much.**

If you are reading this, the chances are very high that you have access to food, water, shelter, clothing, etc. These basics are all anyone really needs. Everything else is gravy.

If you look back over your life, there have probably been times when you had less than you do now. You probably earned less money, had a worse car, or a smaller bed. As you've worked to improve your lot, you've been able to accumulate better quality things, to the point where you wouldn't be happy with those things that were perfectly acceptable to you when you were younger. You probably still want even more.

That's okay. Remember – it's all about your attitude and self-awareness. **You do not need very much.** Don't fall for the hype. Do you really need that designer item or is there something just as good for a fraction of the price? How many pairs of shoes do you really need? And once you've bought those high-end items, how much do you really value them?

The things you value aren't always the most expensive. Look for what's necessary and put your focus there rather than stressing about getting more and more.

5. **True happiness comes from within.**

You might think that money and fame would solve all your problems but you only have to watch shows like *Keeping Up with the Kardashians* to see that it doesn't matter how much wealth and status you have – everybody's problems are still the same. Bill Gates' billions weren't enough to stop him from getting divorced. We all live, love, die. Sure, money might make it easier for you to do things and get what you think what you want, but if you're not happy with yourself, it won't matter how big your bank balance; you will never feel fulfilled.

According to the Stoics, happiness can only be found by living a virtuous life in pursuit of wisdom, justice, self-discipline, and self-awareness.

If you think about the times when you've been happy, *really* happy, it always involves some kind of experience. I bet you can't even remember everything you got for Christmas every year as a child, but you can remember the excitement you felt on Christmas Eve.

Now, this does not mean that wealth is bad, or that money can't buy you things that bring you happiness. Maybe you have visions of living on a yacht because the freedom it will bring you will make you happy…you'll need money to buy that yacht in the first place. However, just because you haven't got that yacht yet doesn't mean you have to wait to be happy. You can experience exactly the same levels of happiness *right now*. A Stoic understands that the really good stuff is to be found in your everyday actions.

6. **Some things matter; a lot of things don't.**
    How many times have you seen something on the news or social media that has made you angry, frustrated, or worried? What did you do? Decide to take a break or continue going back to it, only to feel even more upset?

    Newsflash: the world will not end if you don't keep up with current events. Your friendships will not end if you're not liking every single post 24/7. (And if they do, you probably need better friends.)

    Epictetus said it best: "If you wish to improve, be content to appear clueless or stupid in extraneous matters – don't wish to seem knowledgeable." If someone asks you your opinion on the latest scandal, it's better to reply with "I don't know," or, even better, "I don't care."

    The media wants to make us think that every little thing that's broadcast is incredibly important and maybe it is to those directly affected. But in the grand scheme of things, when you look at it, they don't matter as much as we think we do. If you don't make an effort to keep up with current events, you'll find out about the really important things sooner or later. Yes, you'll probably want to keep up to date with what's impacting your friends and family, but you really don't need to be glued to your phone.

If you want to live a simple life, consider massively cutting back on your social media scrolling. It will free up time and energy for those things that truly matter. And so what if you think you look stupid next time you're out at a party because you don't know the intricacies of the current political landscape? How much does the opinion of others really matter? (As we'll delve into in more depth later in this book, it doesn't matter at all.)

A simple life means being minimalist with your social media.

7. **'No' is a complete sentence.**

It doesn't matter how rich or poor you are, we all only have 24 hours in a day, a finite amount. Doesn't it make sense to spend that precious resource on the important things rather than wasting it on things that don't really matter?

Yet most of us fritter our time away on things that aren't important, neglecting the things that are, such as our families and our health. For most of us, our priorities are all skewed.

It's time to say no to those things that do not serve our highest good. If you don't want to go out, don't go! If you don't want to lend someone your car, don't!

You can also say no to those emotions that aren't helping you, like stress, anger, worry, etc. They rarely help, if at all, and they are just another distraction from what you should actually focus on.

The more you learn to say no and mean it, the more you free yourself to say yes to things that deserve your attention. Rather than going along with what you think you 'should' be doing because that's what society deems important, be Stoic. Use your reason and logic to determine what truly deserves your time and let the trivial things fall away. You'll accomplish so much more if you do.

Living a simple life

If you truly want to live a simple life, you need to move beyond the notion of getting rid of most of your possessions and living a minimalist lifestyle. While a minimalist lifestyle might be simple, a simple life does not have to be minimalist. You may want to become more self-sufficient, growing your own food or going off the grid. There is so much more to life than our possessions, and you can simplify so much more than what you own.

Start by looking at what you believe to be essential. There is no right or wrong answer here; it's all about what *you* value. Is it your relationships, career, belongings, wealth, ambitions? Once you have identified what you believe to be important, look at your relationship with them. Are you making things more complicated than they need to be? Are you creating drama in your life where you don't need to? (Be honest about that one! A lot of what we blame others for originates with ourselves; we just don't want to acknowledge that.)

When you can keep your focus on what you understand to be essential, you'll find that a lot of your existing stresses and strains will simply melt away. There is a basic Stoic principle known as the Dichotomy of Control, which holds that the only thing we can be truly responsible for is what's in our minds. It can be difficult to hold on to this principle when we are so used to making judgments and snap decisions, following our immediate urges without even thinking about it. But when we do this, we misjudge, poor decisions, and end up in situations that cause us harm. All of this can result in stressing about things that aren't worth our energy.

The more you bring yourself back to focusing on what is under your control, the less stressed you'll feel and the easier it will be to make decisions that are the right ones for you, regardless of what anyone else says or does.

So let's say that you have decided to be more minimalist and turn your back on consumerism, keeping only what you need. You may well have friends and family tell you that you're crazy, that you won't be able to sustain a minimalist lifestyle, that you'll regret giving away so much of your stuff. Normally, you might find this kind of criticism difficult to bear, but if you take a step back, you'll be able to see that their comments have no impact on your life other than that which you allow them to have. They are entitled to their opinion, just as you are entitled to ignore it. As soon as you let go of needing the approval of others, life immediately becomes simpler – *and all you've done is change your attitude.*

As Epictetus instructed, *"In the case of particular things that delight you, or benefit you, or to which you have grown attached, remind yourself of what they are. Start with things of little value. If it is china you like, for instance, say, 'I am fond of china.' When it breaks, then you won't be as disconcerted. When giving your wife or child a kiss, repeat to yourself, 'I am kissing a mortal.' Then you won't be so distraught if they are taken from you."*

Whenever something seemingly negative happens, a relationship break-up, say, or losing your job, use the Dichotomy of Control to see if the event was within your control. If it was not, try to allow feelings of loss to pass quickly and instead see it as simply the end of your borrowing something that was never truly yours in the first place.

Be grateful yet detached

Under Stoic principles, detachment and gratitude are two vital ingredients for a simple life. The more you can detach yourself from those things that are temporary and outside of yourself, the more you can be grateful for what you have right now, which makes for a much happier, more contented life.

These two qualities support you to enjoy a simple living lifestyle and, should you choose to be more minimalist, are in direct opposition to consumerism, because they take you away from the urge to Have All The Things so you only pursue that which truly matters. Your levels of happiness are separated from how much you acquire and you feel grateful for what you have, reducing your need to buy more. It becomes a self-sustaining cycle of fulfilment, where you focus on the more important things in life and appreciate them, enhancing your quality of life.

Exercises

Make lists

Make a list of all the things that are truly important to you. Nobody else will be seeing this list, so don't censor yourself as you list out all the things you value and believe to be crucial to your life. This might include your loved ones, family and friends, career, hobbies, spiritual practices, etc.

Now list out what you actually spend your time on. How much time do you spend with the people you care about? How much time do you spend nurturing your career?

And how much time do you spend scrolling social media?

Again, be honest. Nobody is going to judge you because they won't be seeing your list. This is just for you to get a sense of perspective and see where your priorities need to be adjusted.

SECRETS OF THE STOICS

If you want to live a simple life, spend time, not money, on the important things. Money always comes, but once time has passed, you can't get it back. Take control of your time and spend it where you feel it will do the most good.

Prioritize

Now you have your lists, you should have a stronger sense of where you want to spend your time but may not be right now. That's okay. You can shift that.

So let's say that you put 'me time' on your list of things that are important, but looking at your second list, you realize that you hardly ever spend any time on yourself. Now is the time to change it. After all, I bet that if you stepped back and asked yourself why this is, there isn't really a good reason. You've just allowed yourself to fall down on your list of priorities.

Start to change how you do things. Even if you just give yourself five minutes a day, it's a start and once you get into the habit of prioritizing yourself, it becomes easier to do a little more. You might like to meditate – just five minutes a day has been shown to have a positive effect on your physical and mental health, so if you think you can't do much for yourself in five minutes, you're wrong!

After a month of actively determining where you choose your time, repeat the first exercise. You should find that your second list is a little closer to your first. It may not be much, and that's okay. This is a lifelong journey, not an overnight fad, and any progress, no matter how small, will eventually get you where you want to be.

This is why I like to keep all my lists – looking back, I can see how far I've come and it gives me motivation to keep going on those days when I think nothing has changed.

Take control of your habits

We all know that social media is a major time suck. So many of us find ourselves mindlessly scrolling instead of doing what we should be doing. It's one thing to check your social media when you feel like it (and you can always cut back on that), but what about notifications? I don't know about you, but as soon as I hear a 'ping,' I find myself immediately reaching for my phone to find out who's trying to contact me. Once I've checked, yes, you guessed it, I'm off scrolling, even if I checked my social media five minutes ago.

Start to take control of your life and simplify things by switching off notifications. If you can't bring yourself to do this permanently, then set up your phone to only disturb you at certain limited times of the day. If you go the latter route, you could even decide that you'll only check your social media during these times, which will make things even simpler because you have a routine and won't have to give your energy to how many likes or comments you've had all the time.

Summary

The secret to enjoying a simple life is that it's not about a lack of money or possessions, but rather a lack of want and need, a lack of envy, a lack of stress, a lack of insecurity, and a lack of resentment.

- Make a list of what you believe to be important and then another list of where you spend your time right now. Look at the differences between the two for areas you can improve on.
- Spend time, not money.
- Prioritize your activities and spend more time on the things you've determined are valuable.
- Set limits on your social media, which will give you more time and energy for other things while reducing your stress.

HAVE A LITTLE OF WHAT YOU FANCY

Seek not the good in external things; seek it in yourselves.
—Epictetus

The stereotype of a Stoic is of a simple lifestyle, someone who actively deprives themselves of possessions in order to pursue a more moral, fulfilling lifestyle. However, the ancient philosophers were living during a time notorious for wild, decadent parties, orgies, and indulgent festivals, which were the opposite of the Stoic stereotype. So what did they do? Eschew these celebrations in favor of staying home and living a good life?

If that's what you thought, it may surprise you to learn that Seneca, another famous Stoic, possessed no fewer than three hundred tables, which he used solely for his own parties. These were expensive tables, made out of ivory. Seneca could have easily bought ordinary tables, but he chose to treat himself and his guests. Likewise, Cato and Socrates were known for unwinding with a drink, and it is not unreasonable to assume that Marcus Aurelius and Epictetus also had their own luxuries that were important to them.

We've just had an entire chapter focused on how to simplify your life and yet we're now learning that the Stoics *didn't* deprive themselves of at least some of the things they wanted. Isn't that a contradiction in terms?

When you learn a little more about how the ancient Greeks and Romans lived, not only does it make sense, it also teaches an important lesson about how to be more Stoic.

The secret to enjoying a little of what you fancy is to dilute it.

You see, while these days we drink our wine as it comes, pouring it neat from the bottle, the ancient Greeks and Romans would have viewed such behavior as utterly barbaric. Only an undisciplined alcoholic would drink their wine like this.

Instead, the Greeks and Romans would dilute their wine with water. Hesiod, a famous Roman poet, wrote that the best way to enjoy your wine was to mix it with water at a ratio of 1:3. To a modern palate, diluting your wine with three parts water would make it taste weak and unpleasant, not to mention being an insult to the wine itself. But to a Roman, this was the only way to savor wine.

So, rather than being hardened drinkers who were abusing their livers every night, knowing that the ancients diluted their wine, picturing the Stoics sitting down with a watery beverage every evening makes much more sense. This behavior also contains an important lesson for those wishing to be more Stoic.

The Romans and Greeks made very strong wine. Undiluted, it would not take much to make someone drunk. Yet wine was an important drink, something that brought pleasure to the individual, bringing joy to a celebration and helping cement relationships. Mixing water in with the wine is the physical embodiment of one of the most important Stoic virtues: moderation.

So if the last chapter made you worry that you were going to have to give up things you simply don't want to at this point, that's okay. Nobody is telling you that you have to give up anything. But you *can* water down those things that are not serving you or are distracting you from the most important things. Diluting wine in Roman times meant that the taste wasn't so overwhelming, and you could drink for longer without getting drunk. Likewise, diluting those things you know are a distraction means that you can enjoy those things that bring you pleasure without allowing them to distract you from traveling a virtuous path. When you are moderate in your so-called vices, you bring them under your control instead of being at the mercy of always needing more, more, more – and never being satisfied.

Exercises

Know your vices

In order to be more moderate, you first need to be more self-aware. It's time for another list!

Make a list of all the vices, bad habits, or indulgences you have. Think about things that bring you pleasure or you *think* should make you happy. These could be your morning takeout coffee, procrastination, or spending money on upgrades in silly Match 3 games. Big or small, write them all down. There's no judgment here. You're just identifying those habits you have that aren't serving your best self.

Once you have your list, you might look at it and feel overwhelmed. Do you really have to give up all those things?

No, you don't.

In fact, attempting to give up all those 'vices' cold turkey is going to be doomed to failure. It's simply too overwhelming and, what's more, it's not necessary. Later in this book we're going to look into how you should embrace hardship, but, to borrow the theme of this chapter, it's all about moderation. You *can* have those things that bring you pleasure! You just want to be sure that you are in control of those things rather than the other way around. (Caveat: If any of your vices are making you miserable rather than bringing you pleasure, being a Stoic means that you will need to do something about that, but that falls outside the remit of this particular exercise. However, I will say don't be afraid to seek professional help if that's what you feel you need in order to move forward and become more of your best self.)

Once you've listed out your vices, pick one and think about how you can water it down. Do you drink a lot of wine? Consider alternating alcoholic drinks with non-alcoholic ones (there are some good non-alcoholic wines available these days, or be like the Romans and try watering it down). If you've fallen into the habit of drinking every night, start introducing alcohol-free nights and gradually increase the number until you're drinking once a week or less.

Do you find yourself binge-watching Netflix all weekend? Try going out to a movie and spend the rest of your time doing something else. Pick up a good book – maybe something by one of the ancient Stoics to inspire you. If you know that you'll ignore any promises you make to yourself of 'just one more episode,' then try dedicating one weekend a month to binging and make active plans to go out so that you're away from temptation the other weekends.

You can have too much of a good thing. If you're a gym junkie, build in rest days to your routine with active recovery. Do yoga or swimming on alternate days to give your body a rest. You may even find that taking this approach will help your fitness levels even more because your body has time to process after all the hard work of working out.

Be mindful to savor your food

Mindfulness has been shown to help with weight loss, so if you're finding that you have a weakness for sweet treats or you simply eat more than you know you should because it tastes so good, this is a particularly good approach for you.

Mindful eating involves being fully present when you eat. This process can start with preparation, but you can do it with food that someone else made for you. It is very simple: slow down and focus on eating. So many of us multi-task during meals, watching TV while we eat, making a phone call, having a conversation, or reading a book. When you cut out all of that and do nothing but eat, you become far more conscious and aware of what you're doing and get so much more pleasure out of the experience. What's more, you are more likely to stop eating when you're full instead of pushing past because you haven't even noticed you're done.

With every forkful, take a moment to admire your food before putting it in your mouth. What does it look like? How is the aroma? When you finally put the food in your mouth, take a moment to appreciate the texture before eventually chewing it.

Slowing down when you eat your food and really engaging all your senses makes a huge difference to your eating experience. You'll find that a couple of squares of chocolate more than satisfy you, while in the past you could have eaten the whole thing without even blinking.

Being mindful with your food really helps you to be more moderate with it too.

Be moderate with your work

Have you heard the phrase 'Work to live, don't live to work?' It's time to take a good, hard look at your job. Your job is important. There's no doubt about that. It pays the bills and potentially paves the way for you to build the life you want. But it's important to temper your work life with the other important things you have going on. It's all too easy to start spending all your time focusing on work so that by the time you get home, you're too tired to do anything except shovel some food in your mouth and go to bed.

There are a few things you can do to change this. What option you take will very much depend on your own personal circumstances. I understand that not everyone has the freedom to change their hours or get a new job (although that doesn't mean you can't at least make plans to do so.) Work within your current limitations, while understanding that these can always change.

If you are self-employed, make sure you schedule downtime, including at least one day off a week. Yes, you heard me: a day off. When you work for yourself, you can find yourself thinking that the more hours you work, the more money you make. I can tell you from personal experience that this simply isn't true. In fact, I work far fewer hours now than I ever have, yet I make much more money. It's all about working smarter, not harder. And even if you don't change the way you work, you're fooling yourself if you think you can work 24/7 and not have it impact on the quality of your work. If you take just one day off a week, you'll allow your brain to recharge and your body to recuperate, which means you can work so much more effectively on the other days. You'll find yourself more productive and effective in what you do.

If you work for someone else, look at your current situation. Are you spending more hours at the office than you need? Why is that? Is it to get everything done? Or is it really because you want to be *seen* as busy when you could leave earlier?

If you find yourself overworked and constantly struggling to keep up, you need to do something about this. You might talk to your boss about it, think about whether you can delegate anything, or look at how you can streamline your processes.

If you're staying because of the *appearance* of being busy, just stop. Remember – we're not looking for external approval. You can spend all the hours of the day in the office, but you can't control what others think about this. You may even find that others are wondering why it's taking you so long to get everything done. Keep your focus on what's working for you and don't worry about what others are thinking.

How much are you enjoying your job anyway? Is it bringing you happiness and fulfilment or is it making you miserable? What would you do if you could do anything you liked? Once you stop caring about what others think (because it's outside of your control), you'd be surprised at the doors that open up for you. Maybe you always wanted to be a dog trainer, but your parents wanted you to be a lawyer. You might have to accept a drop in pay to follow your dreams, but you'll be so much happier – and you'll be surprised at how much you can make as a dog trainer if you write books, create online courses, etc. You could even find yourself with your own TV show and make more money than you ever did as a lawyer. You simply don't know until you try.

If you don't love your job but you really can't do anything else, at least right now, make sure you moderate it by doing things you *do* love in your spare time. Don't make excuses like *I'm too tired*. Decide that, on Saturdays, you will spend all day doing what you love and sleep all day Sunday if necessary.

Bring more balance into your life in whatever way works for you.

Summary

The secret to enjoying a little of what you fancy is to dilute it.

- Know your vices so you can find healthy ways of enjoying them in moderation.
- Be mindful with your food so you can savor it more while eating less.
- Bring moderation to your work-life balance. What this looks like will depend on your personal situation.

LEARN TO LOVE YOUR LACK OF CONTROL

Don't seek to have events happen as you wish, but wish them to happen as they do happen, and all will be well with you.
—Epictetus

By now it should be clear to you that living a Stoic lifestyle involves a high degree of self-awareness. This path involves taking a long, hard look at your thoughts and behavior so that you can make changes from a powerful place of knowledge.

We've already touched upon the importance of accepting that so much of life is outside of our control and we need to be okay with that. In this chapter, we're really going to dive deep into that principle. It is one of the most fundamental concepts of Stoicism, after all.

Think back to the last time something didn't go your way due to unforeseen circumstances. Maybe the COVID-19 pandemic meant that you couldn't go to a concert you had front row seats for. Perhaps there was really bad traffic on your way to work and you were late for an important meeting. Or maybe there was a heavy snowstorm, and you couldn't go out for a date with someone you really liked.

How did you react? Did you get frustrated and angry? Did you phone the concert organizers and yell at them because they had to cancel the event? Did you blast your horn at the cars in front of you, hoping the noise would make them move, even though there was nowhere for them to go? Did you curse the weather, screaming at the sky to stop snowing?

How did that work out for you? Did it change anything?

Or did you understand that sometimes things happen that are outside our control, and wasting energy on getting upset is a waste when you could spend that energy elsewhere? You might have to miss the concert, but maybe there was an online event you could have attended, or you could save your money for a full VIP experience once it was rescheduled. Maybe you could find an alternate route to work, but if there isn't one, you could use the time sitting in traffic to meditate or listen to an audiobook. The snow might have stopped you meeting your date but Zoom makes it very easy to connect with someone online. Although it's not the same as being with someone in person, you could light a few candles, play some romantic music, and share things you've found online so you can get to know each other better.

There are always options. But if you're getting all worked up, you won't be clearheaded enough to see them. Or, if you do, you won't be able to enjoy them because you'll be obsessing over the things that went wrong.

Next time you find yourself getting angry or upset, take a moment to breathe and ask yourself whether this is actually helping anyone. Is it going to change the situation? Do you have any control over the situation, any at all? If not, is it not true that the only control you have is over yourself and your reaction?

The secret to living like a Stoic is to recognize what is under your control and releasing any attachment to everything else. It is *always* your choice to decide if someone is being hurtful and then allow them to hurt you.

As Epictetus put it, "I must die. Must I then die lamenting? I must be put in chains. Must I then also lament? I must go into exile. Does any man then hinder me from going with smiles and cheerfulness and contentment?" In other words, you choose how you react. Now, it might be difficult to control your reactions in high-stress situations, especially if you are new to a Stoic way of living, but the more aware you can be of this process, the easier it becomes to at least diminish that hurt so that, over time, it becomes less and less until you have complete control over your responses to whatever happens.

Once you take on board the truth of this, you'll find it is incredibly liberating. When you allow someone to upset you, you are giving your power to them. You have bought into their narrative, played their game by allowing yourself to follow their lead. When you appreciate that you **always** have the ability to ignore what someone is saying, or politely respond before removing yourself from the situation, you realize you do not have to accept what they're giving you.

Your life is completely in your hands, no one else's.

The more you can fully embody this principle, the more Stoic you will be. You will be happier and more content because nothing can take away your happiness unless you choose it. Epictetus was a slave for much of his life, but still found happiness. You will learn from some of the other Stoics in this book the challenges they faced but were able to deal with them with equanimity.

Whatever the challenges in your life, you *can* choose to rise above them.

Exercises

Use affirmations

An affirmation is a positive, personal, and specific phrase written in the present tense that you repeat to yourself to reprogram your subconscious to follow your desired way of being. Here are some examples of affirmations you might want to use to release your attachment to anything outside of your control:

- I choose happiness.
- I can only control myself.
- I do not have to allow others to hurt me.
- I do not worry about things that are beyond my power or will.

You might also like to write your own affirmations specific to your situation. Just be sure to keep them positive and in the present tense written in the first person.

A good way of working with mantras is to recite them in front of a mirror. There is something about this mirror work that really helps your subconscious embody what you are telling it, and if your subconscious accepts something as real, everything else falls into line. If that doesn't appeal to you, you can also recite your affirmation in your mind as you go to work or while you're doing the shopping. You can even recite it when confronted with a difficult situation to help you keep your focus on where it should be. You might also like to start and end your day by reciting your affirmation to yourself. You could even use it as a mantra for meditation.

You can support this affirmation work by having reminders about the place. You could print up a number of quotes from Epictetus and display them in your home. Some good ones include:

- If anyone tells you that a certain person speaks ill of you, do not make excuses about what is said of you but answer, "He was ignorant of my other faults, else he would not have mentioned these alone."
- Man is not worried by real problems so much as by his imagined anxieties about real problems.
- It's not what happens to you, but how you react to it that matters.
- Other people's views and troubles can be contagious. Don't sabotage yourself by unwittingly adopting negative, unproductive attitudes through your associations with others.

Use your best self as a guide

I want you to get some paper and write out a description of your best self. Don't limit yourself and don't be constrained by the person you are right now. We can all change and grow; none of us is the person we were a month ago, a year ago, a decade ago. The difference between the you of the past and the you of now is that you are deciding to take control of how that change will look in the future.

So go wild! If the best version of you eats good food, write that down, even if you live off beans on toast. If your best self exercises every day, that goes into your description as well. How does your best self deal with stress? Treat their partner? Their friends? Ignore whatever flaws or any negative self-talk that may come up during this process and really dig deep into what the best version of you is like.

Once you have that description, read it out loud to yourself, in front of a mirror if you like.

Are you ready for the best part of this exercise?

You can be that best self *right now.* You do not have to wait for anything to change. Maybe your best self goes for long walks in the countryside every weekend, but you live in the heart of the city with no means of traveling long distances. That's okay. Find a local park or garden you can walk around in. You don't have to be the *perfect* version of your best self. You just have to be the best you can be!

Another little tip is to ask yourself *What would my best self do?* when you're confronted with a dilemma. You can think back to your description as a guide. If your best self wouldn't have that extra cookie, don't have it! If your best self would make that call to your mom, even though you know she's going to lecture you, make the call with a smile on your face.

The more you allow your best self to guide your choices, the closer you'll become to that best self – and the more you'll reinforce to yourself the fact that you are working on the **only** thing that is under your control.

Now none of us is perfect, so there are bound to be times when you know what your best self would do, but you choose to do the opposite and that's okay. The important thing in this instance is that you are aware that it *is* a choice. As that self-awareness grows, it will become easier and easier to focus on what you can control and move closer towards fully being your best self.

Get some perspective

What would you think if I told you that other people don't think about you half as much as you think they do? It's easy to get caught up in believing that other people are talking about you all the time or coming up with ways to put you down. In fact, I promise you that they'll be far too caught up in their own problems to be spending their time worrying about you. It really is true – out of sight, out of mind. And if you're stressing about the impression you made on someone you just met, the chances are high they're doing exactly the same thing!

We tend towards negative thinking, assuming the worst or ignoring the good. But, as you know now, we have control over our thoughts, so if you find yourself getting stressed over what someone else might be thinking about you, STOP! In the unlikely event that they are wasting energy on you, so what? How is it affecting you in this moment?

When these thoughts come up, question them. Ask yourself, do I know this to be a fact or is it an assumption? And remember, just because someone else has told you something or you've read it on the internet, that doesn't make it true.

Now think about what they might be thinking about instead. If they're not thinking about you, they could be thinking about their latest social media post, a problem at work, what their hair looks like, what to have for dinner, etc. There are so many things someone could be thinking about at any one time that it really is unlikely you're dominating their thoughts.

Now consider their motives if they *are* thinking about you. It's easy to ascribe malicious intent to someone because you want to be negative and then you see everything through that lens until the most innocent of actions becomes a conspiracy. So think about all the possible motives someone might have for thinking about you. Maybe they're worried. Maybe they like you but don't know how to express it. Maybe they feel safe around you and able to vent.

Once you start considering things from someone else's viewpoint, you soon realize that things are rarely black and white or as negative as you assume, so you can let it go and put your focus back to where it's supposed to be – on your own thoughts and actions.

Be your own best friend

Given that you have control over your thoughts and reactions (and nothing else), you have a choice. Do you want that little voice in your head to be your personal cheerleader or do you want it to point out everything that's wrong with you, real or imagined? It's a no brainer, right?

Look, you can't please everyone. You can't make everyone like you. But you *can* please yourself. Focus on making yourself happy first in alignment with your higher best self, and you'll find that you naturally attract the people who make you happy too. When you are comfortable with who you are and have confidence in yourself, people naturally gravitate towards you.

Start paying attention to that little voice in your mind and every time it says something negative, immediately counter it with something positive, preferably with an example that supports your opinion. So if your little voice says, "I can't do this," you immediately come back with "I **can**!"

If your little voice says, "People always let me down," you come back with "No, they don't," and think of a time when someone was there for you (and there will be at least one example in your life.)

If you're having to deal with a problem, let your little cheerleader give you the advice you'd give to a friend in a similar situation *and follow it.*

You cannot rely on anyone else to be your best friend. As we've already discussed, people come and go. But you will **always** be there for yourself – if you allow it.

Summary

The secret to living like a Stoic is to recognize what is under your control and release any attachment to everything else.

- Use affirmations. Keep them positive, in the present tense, and written in the first person.
- Figure out who your best self would be and then let that guide how you live your life.
- Get some perspective. Realize that you might be the center of your universe but the world doesn't revolve around you. You aren't as important to other people as you might think.
- Be your own cheerleader. You are the only person you can rely on. Get control of your thoughts and make them positive and supportive at all times.

PART TWO:

MARCUS AURELIUS

THE LIFE OF MARCUS AURELIUS

Waste no more time arguing about what a good man should be. Be one.

—Marcus Aurelius

Marcus Aurelius was the last of the so-called Five Good Emperors, an epithet given to him centuries after his death by the infamous Niccolo Machiavelli. He was the last emperor of the Pax Romana, which lasted from 27BC to 180AD and was a time of relative stability for the Roman Empire.

We have a lot of evidence about Marcus Aurelius, thanks to the high levels of literacy enjoyed by the Romans. As a consequence, we know a lot about his life and experiences. He was born in Rome on 26 April 121. His father was Marcus Annius Verus, with Roman Italo-Hispanic lineage. His mother was Domitia Lucilla Minor, the daughter of a Roman patrician and wealthy in her own right.

When he was 17, Aurelius was adopted by Antoninus Pius. His birth father had died sometime around 124 when Aurelius was three. The young boy is unlikely to have been able to remember much about his father, but he nevertheless recorded in his *Meditations* that he had learned a lot from what he did remember about him, as well as the things said by others.

His mother did not remarry and it is unlikely that she spent much time with her son, as was the custom among those of her social status. Instead, he was handed over to the care of 'nurses,' along with his grandfather, also called Marcus Annius Verus. Aurelius also wrote about the positive lessons he learned from his grandfather, although he was not so keen on the woman his grandfather took as a partner after his wife died.

Following the fashion among aristocrats of the time, Aurelius was educated at home and publicly thanked Catilius Severus for supporting him to avoid public schools. Another teacher, Diognetus, may have been the one who first introduced Aurelius to a philosophical way of approaching life. In 132, with the encouragement of Diognetus, the future emperor began to dress and live like a philosopher, wearing a rough Greek cloak when studying and, in true Stoic fashion, sleeping on the floor.

Sometime in 132-3 Aurelius started studying with a new set of tutors, including Alexander of Cotiaeum, a Homeric scholar. Aurelius later acknowledged Alexander's influence on his literary style, and subsequent observers have commented on the clear evidence of Alexander's impact on *Meditations*.

Following a brush with death in 136, the then Emperor Hadrian chose Lucius Ceionius Commodus as his successor, despite widespread disapproval. Commodus was in line to become Aurelius' father-in-law and many believed that this move was designed to lead to Aurelius taking over the throne, who was too young at the time to be a named successor. However, Commodus died before Hadrian, so in January 136, Hadrian picked Aurelius Antoninus as his successor. Antoninus was married to Aurelius' aunt and on the command of Hadrian, Antoninus adopted Aurelius. Allegedly, Aurelius was not happy at becoming an adopted member of the ruling family and was reluctant to move from his mother's home to Hadrian's abode, although he obeyed the emperor's wishes.

In 138, Hadrian asked the senate to make an exception for Aurelius so that he could become a quaestor before his 24th birthday. His request was duly granted and thus Aurelius was set on a path that would lead to his becoming emperor.

Hadrian died on 10 July 138 and was buried at Puteoli. Antoninus took up the mantle of emperor, the succession smooth and stable. He left Hadrian's nominees in office and let the senate continue with its business without interference. In addition, he commuted the death sentences of those sentenced in the last few days of Hadrian's rule. As a consequence, he was asked to take the name 'Pius' when he was crowned.

Antoninus asked Aurelius to annul his current engagement to Ceionia Fabia and instead betroth himself to his daughter, Faustina. Aurelius agreed and soon rose in the ranks of the Roman ruling system. Taking the name Marcus Aelius Aurelius Verus Caesar, he moved into the House of Tiberius, the imperial palace, and began to live the life appropriate to his new station. Aurelius was not happy about this, but Antoninus had insisted, and thus began an internal battle between needing to navigate the social mores of court and wanting to pursue philosophy.

In April 145, Aurelius finally married Faustina, who was technically his sister through adoption. Coins were minted to mark the occasion, but Aurelius didn't write much about his marriage in the surviving documents we have from him.

Over the years, Aurelius had been taking instruction from various leading Greek tutors who taught him oratory amongst other classical skills. As a result, Aurelius wrote many of his thoughts in Greek. One of his tutors, Herodes Atticus, was a controversial figure. Fabulously wealthy, he was known for his temper and could be patronizing. He was a vocal opponent of Stoicism and philosophic lifestyles. He claimed that the Stoics would live a "sluggish, ener-vated life." Yet despite his tutor's condemnation, Aurelius came to embrace Stoicism. Notably, he did not mention Atticus at all in his *Meditations*, even though they met many times over the years.

Another tutor, Fronto, had advised Aurelius against studying philosophy and disapproved of his student's sessions with Apollonius of Chalcedon and his peers. Fronto believed that Aurelius had only turned to philosophy because he was bored with his oratory studies. Fortunately for those who came after him, Aurelius ignored Fronto's advice.

While Apollonius may have been the person who introduced Aurelius to Stoicism, it was Quintus Junius Rusticus to whom Fronto attributed as being the one who really drew Aurelius away from ora-tory. Aurelius' philosophical studies were a lifelong endeavor, study-ing under Sextus of Chaeronea in his old age. As he said, "It is good even for an old man to learn; I am now on my way to Sextus the philosopher to learn what I do not yet know."

In 156, Emperor Pius turned 70 and was plagued by ill health. Aurelius had been taking on more and more administrative duties to support the ruler. In 161, Antoninus was at his family estate in Lorium, Etruria. Following a heavy dinner, he vomited overnight and developed a fever the next day. The day after that, he officially passed the state over to Aurelius and died shortly after, ending one of the longest reigns by an emperor.

Following Antoninus' death, Aurelius effectively became the sole ruler of the Empire. While he would have preferred a more philo-sophical life, his Stoic training enabled him to take up the mantle of ruler because it was his duty. However, he refused to accept the role of emperor unless Lucius Commodus was given equal power. Thus, Aurelius became Imperator Caesar Marcus Aurelius Antoninus Augustus, while Lucius took the name Imperator Caesar Lucius

Aurelius Verus Augustus. It was the first time Rome had two emperors. However, although the pair were equal on paper, as the more experienced politician, and the one with the title Pontifex Maximus, Aurelius was clearly the more senior of the two.

The two emperors were very hands on in their rule. When the Tiber burst its banks, flooding Rome and causing widespread famine, the emperors gave the crisis their dedicated personal attention. During other famines, they apparently used the stores in the Roman granaries to provide for those affected.

Throughout all of this, Fronto and Aurelius continued to correspond, with Fronto believing that philosophical lessons were more important than they had ever been. The early days of his reign were highly positive, Aurelius being much loved by his people as a wise and just ruler while continuing his philosophical studies.

Aurelius' reign was not without its difficulties, the first major issue being the war with Parthia. In 161, Vologases IV of Parthia invaded the Kingdom of Armenia, a Roman client state, deposed its king, and installed his own. Under the advice of a prophet, Severianus took a legion into Armenia to reclaim the state, but was easily defeated by general Chosrhoes. Severianus committed suicide, and his men were massacred.

Other areas were also unsettled, including Britain and Upper Germany. Unusual for an emperor, Aurelius had had little preparation for military encounters. He'd spent his time with Antoninus at the former emperor's side rather than in the provinces. Provincial experience, as was usual for future emperors, would have given him valuable experience for dealing with Rome's enemies.

During this time, Fronto proved to be of invaluable support to Aurelius, sending him reading material to broaden his military knowledge and reminding him that Rome had always won out in the end, no matter who the foe.

During the winter of 161-2, word came that rebellion was fomenting in Syria, so Lucius was sent to deal with the Parthian threat in person. Many felt he was more suited to military life because he was the stronger and healthier of the two emperors, but according to Lucius' biographer, the underlying reason for his departure was because he had been too decadent, and it was hoped that the war would tame him a little and make him wake up to the reality of being an emperor. Whatever the reason, in the summer of 162, Lucius left to tackle the situation, leaving Aurelius in Rome to rule the city.

After years of battle, in 165, Roman troops finally recaptured Edessa and returned the original king to power. The Parthians retreated but were pursued by the Romans, who chased them to Mesopotamia. Lucius returned to Rome, victorious.

While Aurelius may have left the Parthian campaign to Lucius, he spent much of his time focusing on matters of imperial administration where he'd already gained a vast amount of experience. He found the theory and practice of legislation interesting, particularly when it came to the manumission of slaves, the fate of minors and orphans, and how city counsellors should be selected. He was respectful towards the Roman Senate and usually asked them for permission to spend money, despite the fact that, as emperor, there was no need to extend such a courtesy. He would remind the Senate that while he might live in the imperial palace, it really belonged to the Senate.

Aurelius died when he was 58 on 17 March 180. We do not know what caused his death, but he was instantly deified, as was common for Roman emperors. He died in his military quarters close to Sirmium, Pannonia, but his ashes were brought back to Rome where they were placed in Hadrian's mausoleum. They stayed there until the Visigoth sack of the city in 410. His military campaigns against the Germans and Sarmatians were commemorated with a temple and column erected in Rome.

Aurelius was succeeded by his son Commodus, a choice which many historians believe was a poor one due to Commodus' unreliability and lack of ability. Iain King wrote, "[The emperor's] Stoic philosophy – which is about self-restraint, duty, and respect for others – was so abjectly abandoned by the imperial line he anointed on his death."

Aurelius had been known as a philosopher king during his lifetime, a title he would retain after his death. Herodian wrote about him, "Alone of the emperors, he gave proof of his learning not by mere words or knowledge of philosophical doctrines but by his blameless character and temperate way of life."

Aurelius was a prolific writer and some of his work still circulates today. His most famous was *Meditations,* which he wrote in Greek during campaigns from 170-80. He would sit down every evening and journal about his thoughts and reflections, which gave a major insight into Stoic philosophy and spirituality. To this day, many still regard it as one of the greatest philosophical works ever written and many leading lights have drawn inspiration from it, including Frederick the Great, John Stuart Mill, and Goethe, as well as more modern figures such as Bill Clinton.

WELCOME AND EMBRACE MISFORTUNE

Here is the rule to remember in the future. When anything tempts you to be bitter: not, 'This is a misfortune' but 'To bear this worthily is good fortune.'
—Marcus Aurelius

L ife is stressful at times. Heck, life can feel stressful *all* the time. This is why Stoicism is gaining in popularity. It helps us to deal with whatever life throws at us. While Marcus Aurelius may not have had to deal with social media, as emperor he was still having to deal with being on call 24/7, navigating the waters of Roman governance and dealing with outside threats and military campaigns. Yet contemporary accounts all talk about Aurelius' positivity and equanimity. How did he manage to keep his calm under so much pressure?

The secret to living like a Stoic is to accept that tough times are a natural part of life, so prepare for them accordingly.

It is well known that modern society is based on lies. The lie that life can be perfect. The lie that you can be happy 100% of the time.

The lie that you can have flawless skin your entire life. Social media has a lot to answer for – filters enable you to present a perfect image to the world while you can choose what to post to create a façade of the dream life.

Anyone who was been a parent of small children will be able to tell you that it is incredibly hard work. Yes, there are those beautiful, heart-warming Hallmark moments, but there's also tears and vomit and sleepless nights and toileting accidents. The reality isn't smooth sailing by any stretch of the imagination, but we all know people who do nothing but post carefully curated photos with captions talking about how blissful it is to be a mother.

Intellectually, we know that life is never picture perfect, but that doesn't stop us from falling for the lie on a deeper level, so we feel driven to keep up and prove that our lives are just as great. Instead of looking inside to do the hard work of self-improvement, we look outside for external validation and then stress ourselves out even more if we don't get it.

So many of us fall into this trap of believing that we are the only ones struggling, even though that simply isn't true. And we do an exceptional job of making ourselves even more miserable as a consequence.

While it is easy to think this is a new phenomenon – after all, social media hasn't been with us very long in the grand scheme of things – these kinds of feelings have been around for millennia. It is such an old problem that the Stoics devised a solution for it. They realized that one of the main reasons we are unhappy is because we always seem to want more than we have. No matter how many achievements we may have or how big our bank balance, we're always wanting more, more, more. Yet the reason why we want more is because we're looking to have a better life.

At what point are you going to wake up to the fact that it doesn't matter how much you accumulate – happiness comes from within?

We're all under a lot of pressure to conform and keep up with the Joneses. It can be hard to resist the urge to get the latest iPhone or jump onto the latest social media trend, but that pressure to follow the herd is one of the main reasons you're unhappy and are constantly searching for something else.

Compare that to the ancient Stoics. They actively followed a simpler lifestyle, which we covered in an earlier chapter, one in which they kept their focus on the important things in life and let everything else fall away. Aurelius wrote, "When someone is properly grounded in life, they shouldn't have to look outside themselves for approval." There's a lot of self-discipline involved in ignoring what everyone else is doing, but there's also a lot of self-fulfilment and when you start doing what makes *you* happy, funny enough, to become happier!

If choosing to walk your own path without being influenced by others seems daunting, that's okay. It's a lifelong journey. But one of the ways in which you can make this easier for yourself is to learn to develop resilience during difficult times.

Many of the Stoic philosophers put a great deal of attention on the question of why bad things happen, no matter how good or virtuous a person you are. They eventually decided that it didn't matter who you were; inevitably you would come up against difficulties. As such, it was important to have the ability to cope when the tough times hit. As Aurelius put it, "When jarred, unavoidably, by circumstance revert at once to yourself and don't lose the rhythm more than you can help. You'll have a better grasp of harmony if you keep going back to it." Being yourself no matter what will help you stay strong.

Another quote from Aurelius' *Meditations* states, "Here is a rule to remember in future, when anything tempts you to feel bitter: not 'This is misfortune,' but 'To bear this worthily is good fortune.'" While those challenges might not be pleasant, ultimately it is our hardships that enable us to grow. They teach us our potential (which is frequently far greater than we give ourselves credit for) and show us where our limits lie. They teach us so much about ourselves that we simply wouldn't otherwise know.

According to Stoic principles, when you have found inner peace, whatever happens to you is irrelevant. You can maintain a calm composure. Or, as Aurelius said, "Very little is needed to make a happy life; it is all within yourself, in your way of thinking."

Given all of this, it is clear that it is important to focus on your inner tranquillity long before anything negative occurs so that when something bad happens, you have the ability not just to deal with it but actively take the situation and transform it into something positive. To use one of Aurelius' metaphors, "As a blazing fire takes whatever you throw on it and makes it light and flame."

When you step back and look at the big picture, the only reason we label something as negative or positive is because of our perception and prejudices. When we move away from that and take a more balanced view, we can see the good and bad in *every* situation. There are always two sides of the coin in whatever happens, offering multiple life lessons if we choose to learn them. When we embrace any situation as a learning opportunity, we can cope with anything that happens.

It could be argued that it is impossible to be Stoic without an element of misfortune. Those difficulties allow us to become more virtuous and thus better people. Viewed in this manner, bad things happen to good people because they give them a chance to build an even better character.

The Stoics took this concept to its logical conclusion, by spending a certain amount of time actively courting hardship. Even though he was destined for a life of high status, Aurelius put this idea into practice, such as when he chose to wear a rough cloak while studying and forgoing a bed to sleep on the floor. This attitude undoubtedly is what made Aurelius such an empathetic ruler and so beloved by all – he didn't hesitate to help feed the people in times of famine, while other leaders might have hoarded the food for themselves and their closest allies.

Another Stoic philosopher, Seneca (whom we will be looking at later in this book), advised people to actively choose to put themselves in tough situations. A wealthy man, Seneca believed that choosing to live as if you were poor helped you to understand what others might be going through and helped build character. Some of his choices were rather extreme, including limiting the food he ate, only wearing old, threadbare clothes, and even sleeping on the streets. While I am not recommending you go this far, there is still a lot to be said for placing yourself in a situation where you do not have access to all the luxuries of your day-to-day life. When you choose to be in a situation that would be your worst nightmare, you remove the power it has over you. You no longer dread the possibility because you've realized you can experience it and still survive.

This is where the practical aspect of Stoicism comes in. You cannot simply meditate on what it might be like to lose your job or have your home repossessed (although this is a useful exercise). You need to actively experience what it would be like to have no money or lose your possessions so you can appreciate them while you still have them.

Many of us feel trapped in a job we hate but we keep going to work because we fear what would happen if we don't. What if we can't pay our bills? What if others judge us for giving it up for something that makes us happy instead? Once you experience first-hand what life would be like if you did lose your job, it's less frightening.

It may even inspire you to quit your job in favor of something more fulfilling.

Living a Stoic life teaches you to lean into misfortune. If your life really is perfect, create a difficult situation for yourself so that if the worst ever did suddenly happen, you could cope instead of crumbling under the pressure.

It's worth noting that we never worry about the past. It has already happened. We know how it panned out and we don't stress because it's done. We worry about the future because it's unknown. Anything can happen. This fear of *what if* can be so terrifying it becomes crippling. Facing this fear on your own terms frees you from its grip, as well as enabling you to come up with various ways of tackling the situation.

Even if you hit absolute rock bottom, there's still a positive to be found – the only way forward is up. The only certainty in life is change. This too will pass.

There are some really simple ways you can challenge yourself. Some of us are so addicted to our phones that we can't bear the thought of being without them. Some of us can't even contemplate the idea of going out without makeup or looking our very best.

What would happen if you locked your phone away for a few days so you couldn't access it? What would happen if you went out in old, shabby clothing?

Not an awful lot. Life would go on. You may even find that you're surprised by how people respond to you in a more natural look or the opportunities that arise to fill your time when you aren't glued to your phone.

Just little steps like this are a way of easing yourself into a Stoic lifestyle and shifting your perspective to one of detachment and gratitude. Social media can be particularly insidious when it comes to trying to be more Stoic. Through the wonders of the internet, we are constantly connected to the rest of the world, which means that our time is rarely ours because we're giving it away to social media. Even on vacation, the time when we're supposed to be relaxing and unwinding, most of us are still in contact with home or even work via text, instant message, or email.

When was the last time you simply sat with yourself? Took some time to look inwards to figure out who you are and who you want to be? Social media is a distraction from the important work of self-reflection. When you step back, you can get a taste of who you might be if you chose to ignore other people's opinion of you and only cared about what you thought about yourself.

When you actively opt for giving yourself a break from your devices, you can also appreciate how lucky you are to have access to the technology you have. Not everyone has a tablet or phone. Not everyone has access to the internet. For some people, these are new innovations, and they remember what life was like without them and how much easier things might have been with modern technology back then. It is a huge privilege to be able to speak to someone whenever you like, wherever you are. Not everyone has that ability. Taking a break from your phone or social media will help you appreciate this.

If you choose to deprive yourself of something but make a big deal out of it, telling everyone you're doing so they can applaud you for your sacrifice, you're not being Stoic. The purpose of this exercise is to become more self-disciplined and self-reliant. It can also help you with leading a simpler life because it gives you the chance to think about what you really need and what motivates you to do the things you do.

To a Stoic, the real misfortune is when someone kids themselves into believing foolish things are important. If you think that happiness is found in your bank balance, you are going to spend your life being miserable and disappointed. There's always more wealth to acquire, people with more than you. Choosing to be more disciplined and making things harder than they need to be will help you discover who you truly are and where your priorities lie, and enable you to be satisfied with your life, whatever happens.

Exercises

Practice misfortune on a regular basis

You can practice misfortune as a one-off when inspiration hits you, but if you want to effectively develop a Stoic mindset, you need to be actively courting hardship on a regular basis, whether that's daily, weekly, or monthly. You should choose something that pushes you out of your comfort zone, something you find challenging and scary, or represents a situation you hope never happens, or makes you stay up at night, worrying.

Here are some suggestions to get you started, but feel free to use your imagination to come up with ideas that will work best for you:

- **Fast.** If you are fit and well, you might like to try fasting for 24 hours once a month. Make sure you drink more water than usual to compensate for the loss of fluids from food and you will find that you can do without food for a day (although I would advise that you check with a medical professional first).
- **Eat a boring, restricted diet.** Limit your choice of food for a short period of time - say, a week or two. Pick something bland, such as bread and cheese, or rice and beans, and eat nothing but that for a short period. While this is not a sustainable diet in the long term, cutting your food back to the

bare minimum to subsist on will allow you to see that you can cope with very little if you must

- **Put together your outfits from charity shops.** If you're someone who takes pride in their appearance and always has to keep up with the latest fashion trends, this is a good thing to try. Go to a charity shop and decide that you're going to put together an entire outfit, head to toe, with just what you find in the shop, no matter how limited the selection. I would advise you choose clothes that are outside of what you would normally wear – you can find amazing items in charity shops and if you come out feeling like you look incredible, it defeats the Stoic purpose of the exercise!

- **Volunteer.** Having shopped in a charity shop, you might decide to volunteer your services. So many charities are always looking for people to help out and if you take a hands-on role, you get a chance to see what life is like for others. You might like to work at a food bank, soup kitchen, or animal shelter, but whatever you choose, remember the principle of going outside your comfort zone. If you love animals, for example, don't work at a shelter. Choose something more challenging for you.

- **Limit your spending money.** How much money do you have to spend after you've paid your bills? However much it is, halve it and live off that for a month. Take out cash and once you've spent it, that's it. Don't withdraw any more. Notice how this limits your lifestyle. Pay attention to the adjustments you have to make to survive on less.

- **Have cold showers.** If all of the above suggestions seem too overwhelming, start small and start having cold showers. For many of us, there's nothing more luxurious than a wonderfully hot shower. Cut out the hot water from your life. After all, if you can't pay your power bill, you can't have a hot shower, so this will give you a little insight into what life could be like if you lost your job.

Start from scratch every time you go on vacation

This exercise is inspired by the Austrian writer, Stefan Zweig. As a young man, he roamed the world, and he took this as an opportunity to prepare for future hard times. So, when he arrived in a new place, he'd pretend that he'd recently moved there. He had no friends in this new place and urgently needed a job to pay the bills. He'd go around all the stores asking if any were hiring. He'd browse newspaper ads to see who was looking for staff.

There were a number of times when he'd follow through right to when he received an offer of employment. Having achieved his goal of proving he could start from nothing, he'd turn down the offer and go off and enjoy his holiday, secure in the knowledge that were he ever in a position where he really didn't have anything, he could figure something out.

Make a fool out of yourself

It might be that you aren't afraid of losing your physical possessions or being homeless. It may be that your biggest fear is about being judged by others. In this instance, it might be hard to think of ways you can practise misfortune.

You're going to need to push yourself outside your comfort zone. Deliberately fall over in front of someone whose opinion you value. (You'll probably find they're more concerned about your wellbeing than thinking about criticizing you!) Go to a club and dance like nobody's watching. (They're probably not.) Take up a hobby that has always interested you but you've been afraid to try because you think it's going to be too hard, something challenging such as silver smithing, pottery, archery. If you're the kind of person who has to be perfect at everything, see what it's like to be bottom of the class for once. You could even sign up for a class and deliberately flunk it to experience what it's like to fail.

Accept your feelings without judgment

As you start to actively practice misfortune, you may find that some things make you deeply uncomfortable. You may even find that you dislike it so much that you can't maintain a particular exercise – *and that's okay.* Your feelings are your feelings. This is part of the learning process.

Take the time to examine why you feel this way. What is it about the exercise that disturbs you so much? Why are you finding it so hard? This is all about the process of self-discovery. As you unpack your emotions surrounding a particular situation, you learn more about yourself and you can find ways to develop coping mechanisms so that, lest you be in this situation for real, you will be able to deal with it more effectively.

Summary

The secret to living like a Stoic is to accept that tough times are a natural part of life, so prepare for them accordingly.

- Actively practise misfortune, whatever that may look like for you. Choose to deprive yourself of some of the things you worry about losing to build resilience in the event of future hardships.

- Use your vacations as an opportunity to discover what you would do if you had to start again with nothing.
- If you need the approval of others, find ways of making a fool of yourself. Really put yourself in your worst nightmare to remove the hold it has over you.
- Accept your feelings without judgment. These exercises are designed to make you feel uncomfortable and you may find this difficult to bear when you first start. Accept how you feel, whatever that may be, and take it as an opportunity to learn more about yourself.

JOURNAL EVERY DAY

*"The happiness of your life depends upon the quality
of your thoughts"*
—Marcus Aurelius

Marcus Aurelius wrote one of the most important philosophical texts of all times, yet his *Meditations* was never intended for public consumption. Instead, they were collected together from his daily journaling practice, when he sat down every day to record his thoughts and observations. It is worth noting that he addressed his meditations as being "to himself."

Many of the ancient Stoics kept journals. Epictetus instructed his students to "write down day by day" their philosophical insights to "exercise themselves." Seneca was reported as saying that he wrote in his journal after his wife had retired for the night to "examine my entire day and go back over what I've done and said, hiding nothing from myself, passing nothing by." Allegedly, this practice enabled him to sleep particularly soundly.

Journaling is a different process than keeping a diary. A diary records the events of the day to keep a note of what's happened. A journal dives deeper, reflecting on those events and delving deep into any insights that may have occurred.

The secret to journaling like a Stoic is to consider what has happened to you on any given day and make note of the lessons you have learned. You should also look forward to the next day and consider how you can prepare yourself for what might happen. This will help you progress faster along your Stoic journey and support you to get even more out of the experience. As we have discussed, Stoicism is a practical philosophy, so it is not enough to read books about Stoicism. You need to actively reflect on what you learn from those books and find ways of incorporating those lessons into your daily life.

A journal can help you identify where you have been Stoic and where you need to do more work. You can use your journal to highlight any sections of Stoic books that have particularly resonated with you and explore those concepts in greater depth.

Journaling also helps you to watch your progress, which will motivate you to keep going with your Stoic life. Sometimes we can feel like nothing has changed, especially if we're having a tough day. A journal enables you to look back and see how far you've come.

Developing a journaling practice

If you are not used to journaling, it can be difficult to build this into your daily routine. This is where you need to be disciplined – but there are ways of making this easy for yourself.

First, you don't *have* to write with pen and paper. You'll hear many people advising you to keep a paper journal because the process of writing by hand forces you to slow down and really focus on what you're doing. While this is true, for some people, handwriting simply isn't fun or comfortable, so don't do it! If you prefer, feel free to use your laptop, desktop, or even phone for your journal. If this makes the words flow and your thoughts come out with ease, don't be afraid to type. After all, this is your journal, not a class assignment. You should do what works for you without worrying about anyone else.

Experiment with what works for you. Don't assume that you won't like a handwritten journal until you've tried it. Try downloading a journaling app with daily prompts to get you going.

Make time to journal. Build it into your daily routine. Just as you brush your teeth and get dressed every day, so should journaling become something you do automatically. When you start, you might find it helpful to actively schedule time into your day for your journal and stick to it no matter what. It's very easy to say you'll journal later but before you know it, you're tucked into bed and you've skipped your journaling for yet another day.

Even if you're not in the mood, you need to journal. I find that journaling always has a positive impact on how I'm feeling, no matter how uninspired I am, so I push through those moments when I just don't feel like it.

You could pair your journaling with another activity, like your first cup of coffee in the morning or before you settle down to unwind with Netflix at the end of the day. You'll hear a lot about Morning Pages, which is when you sit down first thing and write three pages of A4 with whatever comes to mind. This can be a brilliant exercise – but not for everyone. Not everyone feels like doing anything until they've had a chance to properly wake up and their brain is in gear. If you're not a morning person, that's okay. Journal in the evening. There are a lot of positives about journaling first thing, when you can plan out your day and decide what you want to get done, but there's also a lot of value to be had in reflecting back on events.

I'll say it again: this is **your** journal. Write in it at a time which suits **you** best, no one else.

Don't pressure yourself. If you're not used to journaling, it's going to take a while for your journaling routine to establish itself. While it might take as little as 18 days for someone to form a new habit, it can also take as long as 254 days, with an average of 66 days for a behavior to fully integrate and become automatic. So start small and be realistic with your expectations. It is more important to journal every day than it is to write reams and reams of pages. If 10 minutes of journaling seems like a chore, cut it back to five, or even two If you only write a single sentence, that's okay. It might be the most insightful sentence ever written. When you get started, your focus should be on establishing the routine. Everything else is gravy.

You might find it helpful to track your journaling. There are apps that allow you to track your habits, so you can tick off when you've journaled for the day and watch those little marks build up until, before you know it, you've got a few months behind you.

It's funny how something as silly and simple as ticking a box every day can make a difference, but it really does. Knowing that you'll be breaking a chain can be all the motivation you need to write in your journal for just a couple of minutes when you don't feel like it. And once you've started, the chances are high you'll want to keep going.

Get a journal that suits your personal style. I'd advise getting one small enough for you to be able to carry it with you. If you prefer having a larger one to let your thoughts run free, you may even want to have a second one to keep with you at all times if you are concerned about others seeing the personal thoughts in your main journal.

When you have a journal available at all times, you can use it to help you keep on your Stoic path. Maybe you find yourself in a situation that would normally make you angry, but your new attitude has helped you keep your cool and you want to write about this in the moment while everything's fresh. Having your journal with you enables you to do this.

If you're taking a break from your phone, a journal can be a good distraction as well. It gives you something to do with your hands and something to focus on when you're waiting to be called for an appointment.

Whether you have one or two (or even more!) journals, make them personal to you. You might like to get a beautiful notebook that is a pure joy to write in. You might find something like that intimidating and prefer a simple A4 notepad, which is nothing special to look at but gives you plenty of space to explore your thoughts.

Don't get hung up on presentation. Your journal is for your eyes only, so if your handwriting isn't great, don't worry. There's a good chance you haven't done anything for a while and you're out of practice. It'll get better with time. The **only** thing that matters is that you journal, not how it looks.

Find ways of making journaling a treat you look forward to. You might like to have a favorite pen you save just for your journal, or you could make yourself a tasty hot drink before curling up with your book. Put on some music you love or light some incense. You can use this time to really treat all the senses so your thoughts flow freely.

Nobody can journal freely if they're writing for someone else. Keep your journal in a safe and secure place where no one else will find and read it. If you don't have anywhere appropriate, you might like to keep your journal hidden behind a password on your laptop.

Above all, keep your journaling positive. We've already discussed how the only thing you can control are your thoughts. Your journal is an excellent way to help you maintain a positive, balanced mindset and assess events from a detached perspective. While it can be incredibly therapeutic to rant in your journal and let everything out, without a positive solution or analysis of what you can do better in the future (and only you as the only thing you can control), your journal will not be supporting you in the way you want. It certainly won't be Stoic.

Exercises

Start a journal

It should be no surprise that the first exercise for this chapter will be to start your journal. If this thought makes you feel uncomfortable, view this as a great opportunity to welcome misfortune and do something that challenges you.

Decide on whether you're going to keep a handwritten journal or use one of your devices. Buy yourself a nice notebook and pen if you feel it will motivate you to write.

Then write. It can be as little as one sentence a day, which can be a very interesting exercise. How can you encapsulate the last 24 hours in just a few words?

Or maybe write down the most significant event of the day, even if it's something you think someone else would find meaningless, and then analyze what you've learned from it.

Evaluate your journey into Stoicism

Once a week, take time to look back over the last seven days and review your progress. Where have you been Stoic? Where do you need to do more work? Maybe you've set yourself some goals. This is a good time to check your progress and reassess your priorities. Think about the biggest lesson of the week and note how this has impacted you. This will really help you see how Stoicism is having a positive effect on your life.

Collect journaling prompts

There are as many different ways to keep a journal. You might like to use the same prompts every day, or you might like to mix things up. Or, if you've been using the same prompts, you might find yourself getting bored after a while, so using new prompts will help keep things fresh.

Start collecting prompts, either in your notebook or in a document on your laptop or phone, so you've always got something to write about, even on those days when you're feeling particularly uninspired.

You can find plenty of prompts online, but here are a few to get you started:

- Describe an important event from the past 24 hours. How did you behave? How do you wish you had behaved? Would you change anything? What did you learn?
- Open up a book at random (perhaps one by a Stoic author?) and write down the first sentence that jumps out at you. Now write your reflections on that sentence.
- Make a list of goals you would like to work towards. These could be related to your career or finances, but they could also be about your relationships with the people around you – partner, children, parents, friends, colleagues, etc. – your

spiritual practices, or anything else of importance. Now think about what you can do to make those dreams a reality or things you've already done.

If in doubt, write about gratitude

We've discussed the importance of gratitude in being Stoic. Gratitude is an excellent subject for your journal because it can really help you develop a resilient mindset to get you through the toughest times. Focusing on the positive makes you see that there is always something to be grateful for and helps you appreciate that there are always good things coming your way.

You might like to finish your journaling session with three things you feel grateful for, but if you really want to dig deep into gratitude, a helpful exercise is to set a timer for five minutes and list as many things as you can think of without stopping. If you're struggling to come up with things, you can note different parts of your body that you're grateful for (your hands, which allow you to write; your feet, which carry you all day; etc.), or look around the room and be grateful for all the things you see. If you want to really supercharge your gratitudes, you can add a reason *why* you're grateful for the things you're listing.

Alternatively, when you list something you're grateful for, describe the emotions you're feeling. Don't just focus on the surface level, but think about how that item makes you feel. What do you associate with it? Do you have any positive memories you want to explore?

Gratitude journaling is especially useful when you're feeling down. It can help you identify solutions or give you the courage to make a change once you remind yourself that there are always things to be grateful for.

Experiment with different journaling techniques

If you're struggling to get into journaling, it may just be that you're not using the best technique for you. There is no right or wrong way to journal. The most important thing is that it serves your needs. The how really isn't relevant.

You can do a Google search for inspiration, but a few different methods you might like to explore include:

- **Free writing.** Set a timer and write down whatever occurs to you in a stream of consciousness. Do not edit or censor yourself; just let whatever's going to come out, come out. This can be a really useful exercise to unearth thoughts you may not have been fully aware of.

- **Unsent letter.** As the name would suggest, write a letter to someone with all the things you wish you could say to them. You may like to take this as an opportunity to forgive someone who hurt you. This is a very powerful, liberating exercise and remember that just because you have forgiven someone doesn't mean that you have to let them hurt you again. It is okay to keep them out of your life if that's what's healthy for you.

- **Brainstorming.** If you have a problem that seems overwhelming, try brainstorming all the possible solutions, even the really unique ones you wouldn't usually consider. You might be surprised by what comes up.

- **Make a to-do list and prioritize it.** This can be a list focused on your long-term goals or whatever you want to get done tomorrow. Figuring out the things you need to do to achieve a goal can help that goal seem more achievable, or if you know you have a busy day ahead, prioritizing your tasks can make it feel less overwhelming.

- **Lists.** If you're really uninspired, lists are a good way of keeping up your journaling habit without getting too heavy. List the shows you want to watch on Netflix, the books you want to read, the things you'd put on your bucket list. Anything you feel inspired to write about.
- **Worst case scenario journaling.** We'll explore this concept more in a later chapter, but a very Stoic practice was to consider the absolute worst that could happen and prepare for it. Write down something that frightens you and then examine all the possible outcomes and ways you could deal with it.

Assess your journaling on a regular basis

Your journaling needs to work for you. Because Stoicism involves a high degree of self-awareness, you should review your journaling as much as you do every other aspect of your life.

Think about what you want to get out of your journaling and then examine your journal to see if it is fully serving that purpose. You could do a journaling session about your journaling experience. Is it still fun? If not, why not? What do you think you can change to make it more enjoyable? How do you feel at the end of a journaling session? Invigorated or glad it's over?

You want to keep up your journaling practice, so if it's not doing what you need it to do, evaluating your process before you quit is a good way to help you stay on track. Even a little change like switching up the time of day you journal can make a huge difference, but you won't know that you need to do it if you don't take some time to self-reflect.

Summary

The secret to journaling like a Stoic is to consider what has happened to you on any given day and make note of the lessons you have learned. You should also look forward to the next day and consider how you can prepare yourself for what might happen.

- Start journaling!
- Use your journal to chart your progress along the path to Stoicism.
- Collect journaling prompts so you are never stuck for something to write about.
- Gratitude is always a good topic for your journal.
- Experiment with different journaling techniques.
- Review your journaling process on a regular basis to ensure it's still working for you.

TURN THE OBSTACLE UPSIDE DOWN

"The impediment to action advances action.
What stands in the way becomes the way"
—Marcus Aurelius

n this chapter we are going to dive into one of the most fundamental Stoic principles, the notion of using an obstacle to inspire you to greater action, or turning the obstacle upside down. You may be familiar with this idea, thanks to Ryan Holiday's book, *The Obstacle Is the Way: The Timeless Art of Turning Trials into Triumph*, which was inspired by this concept. As is always the case with Stoicism, this is a practical way of living, which needs to be put into practice rather than simply studied.

The secret to living like Marcus Aurelius is to take a negative and transform it into a positive.

In simple terms, turning the obstacle upside down means finding the opportunity hidden within what would seem on the surface to be a negative situation. If you take the right perspective, there is *always* positive to be found in any negativity. There are lessons to be learned, which help us grow as people. So we should embrace the hardship (just as we discussed earlier) and allow it to inspire us to greater heights.

If you lose your job, this is the perfect opportunity to find one which suits you better. (And no matter how much you loved your job, there's *always* a better one out there.) You could find one that pays better, has a nicer boss, or opens up promotion prospects. You could change direction and follow your passions. You could even take some time out and be home with your family for a while.

If you are working with someone you find incredibly annoying, this is an opportunity for you to be creative in how you deal with other people. It can teach patience and empathy. You may discover further down the line that your colleague has been dealing with a difficult personal issue, which is why they've been behaving the way they have; a little compassion could make a huge difference to them.

If you are having difficulties with your partner, this is an opportunity to really consider what you want from them. It allows you to examine your priorities and whether you are with the right person for you. You cannot control their thoughts or behavior, but you can look at what you are doing to contribute to the situation. You can look into different ways of connecting with your partner, which could end up bringing you even closer than ever before. Frequently, when a couple comes out on the other side of a rough patch, they find that their relationship is stronger for having worked through it together.

And if your relationship does end, it means that you were not with the right person anymore, no matter how much in love you may have been in the past. This is an opportunity to find someone who is a better fit for you, which will be easier now that you have higher levels of self-awareness, thanks to your Stoic approach to life.

If you have been practising the elements you've been learning about in this book, by now you should understand that it really doesn't matter what life throws at you. You have no control over anything other than how you react. Release yourself from any desire to try and control what is going on and avoid placing any value judgments on what happens. There is no such thing as a positive or negative situation. There are merely learning opportunities, with obstacles put in your path to teach you how you can be creative in moving past them, helping you grow, becoming the best version of you, and living in harmony with the natural tides of life.

As Aurelius wrote, "Is your cucumber bitter? Throw it away. Are there briars in your path? Turn aside. That is enough." Do not go on and ask, "Why were things of this sort ever brought into this world?"

Aurelius was a Roman emperor, one of the most stressful roles anyone can have. His Stoicism enabled him to be an effective leader, one of the Good Emperors, and his approach has survived the test of time. If you look at any successful leader or entrepreneur, you'll notice one simple truth: they will make the most of every single opportunity that comes their way. Moreover, they make their own opportunities. But most importantly, for every success, there are multiple failures for which they are grateful because of the lessons they learned and the unexpected doors that opened for them.

As they say, an overnight success happens after years of hard work, blood, sweat, and tears. When you adopt a Stoic mindset, you gain the ability to see opportunity in any situation. You accept that bad things are just as likely to occur as good, but they contain just as much potential as the positive – more, even – as not only do bad things bring opportunity for change with them, they also have valuable life lessons to teach.

This is why a Stoic would argue that there is no such thing as good or bad. These value judgments are solely the result of your perception, and you always have the ability to change your perception.

For example, if your relationship ends, you might feel like you'll never find love again and lock yourself away from the world, burying yourself in a huge tub of ice cream. Or you might decide that this is a sign that that person wasn't right for you and allow yourself some time to mourn the relationship but go out and have fun, with no pressure on yourself to find a new romance. Which response is more likely to help you find your true soulmate?

Nobody is saying that you can't feel sad or upset when something negative happens to you. These are normal human responses to a bad situation. But you have a choice over whether you allow these feelings to linger or you let them wash over you and drift away because you're focused on all the opportunities to meet new people. You might even start to look at your previous relationship and see all the ways in which it wasn't working for you. Maybe you wanted to do a particular activity, but your partner wasn't interested but wouldn't let you do it without them. Well, now you can go out and do it!

There are three steps you can take to help you make the most of any situation: change your perception; take action; and follow your true path.

Perception

Your perception is how you personally interpret and react to events around you and what happens to you. Perception has an incredibly powerful influence on you – it completely defines how you experience everything and anything. It's why some people like you and others don't – they see different qualities in you, or where they see the same qualities, they interpret them in different ways. Change that perception and you can instantly make a friend or an enemy.

It is said that the universe gives you more of what you focus on. Perception plays a huge part in this. Let's say that you decide you would like to buy a yellow car because they are rare. Suddenly, you see yellow cars everywhere you go. It's not that there are more yellow cars than there used to be. You are just choosing to see them now.

This means that if you choose to focus on the things that annoy or upset you, this is what you'll pay attention to and you'll miss all the wonderful things in your life. Complain about the rain and you won't see the rainbow.

The first stage in turning the obstacle upside down is to free yourself from your emotions. This is easier said than done. So many of us think that we have no control over how we feel, but in fact, if you master the art of shaping your perception to serve your needs, you'll discover that your emotions naturally fall in line.

If you are a pessimist, inclined to only seeing the worst in events or people, you'll need to take a step back from your prejudices and expectations to be more objective so you can see things as they truly are.

So that annoying colleague becomes less irritating and as a consequence, you're able to hold a conversation with them, which is when you learn about the difficulties they're dealing with at home. This bigger-picture view then enables you to be more patient the next time they do something to aggravate you.

Action

Whatever you do, you are taking action. Even if you do absolutely nothing, this is still a type of action that comes with its own set of consequences. This makes it important to choose the right action for any given situation.

We are all taking action all of the time. However, most of us are taking action without thinking about it. If you are to be Stoic in your thoughts and behavior, you need to take control over your actions, ensuring that whatever you decide to do has a purpose and aim. Doing nothing can be incredibly purposeful if you decide that the best reaction is to wait and see how things change, gathering information before taking your next step.

Choosing the right action involves taking a long-term view so that you can be certain that every choice you make serves your highest purpose. So, if you want to be a lawyer, but you find yourself working in sales, you need to have the courage to leave your job and find a position that takes you closer to where you want to be instead of being miserable for the sake of paying the bills. There are many ways to get to where you want to go. It may be that you get work as a paralegal and study law in the evenings so you can qualify. Or, you go back to university as a mature student and study part-time so you can continue to work to support your studies.

Being Stoic in your actions means that you take control of your life instead of letting life control you. The only way of dealing with your problems is to take action and you have the power to take the *right* action.

Find your true path and follow it

Under Stoic thought, everyone has a purpose in life. When you find your true path and follow it, nothing will stand in your way.

However, it can be difficult to determine what your true path really is. Most of us haven't got a clue what we were put on this earth to do – and that's okay. It's all part of the journey and the very process of discovering your life path is an important lesson in and of itself.

There is an exercise about finding your true path at the end of this chapter, but before we go into that, I want to discuss something very important: what you 'will' as opposed to what you 'want.' Your will is your true calling, the thing(s) you are meant to be doing. Your want is, well, what you want! It is easy to fall into the trap of thinking that just because you really want something or someone, this is what you 'should' have. However, sometimes we want things that aren't right for us or people who aren't healthy for us to be around. Just because we want something doesn't mean it is the best thing or that there isn't better out there. Further, if you're going after something just because you want it, you leave yourself open to being disappointed when it doesn't work out the way you think it will (and it rarely does if it isn't your true path). You are allowing yourself to be ruled by your desires instead of pursuing a virtuous life, the very opposite of what a Stoic should be.

Even when you have found your calling, it may not be possible for you to make it happen right now. There may well be life lessons you have to learn first and this is where turning the obstacle upside down really helps.

If you can only see negative options in your future, following your will allows you to see them all as learning experiences designed to get you to where you need to be. You accept where you are and appreciate it for what it is rather than yearning to be somewhere else.

If you are to be truly Stoic, you need to embrace whatever happens in life and always look for the lessons and opportunities that surround you.

Exercises

Change your perception

Stop what you're doing and look around you. Pay close attention to where you are. Even if you're somewhere really familiar, there will be things you haven't noticed before – maybe the way a certain shadow falls or how something is slightly out of place.

Now pick an item, anything you like. What it is doesn't matter. Focus your attention on it to the exclusion of everything else around you. As you look, you'll notice it shifting in its appearance. Maybe the colors become brighter, the things around it fading away as it comes forward. This item is now the most important thing in your life in this moment.

Imagine that you *are* this item. What can you see from your new perspective? What does the surrounding area look like? Can you see yourself sitting there, looking at the item?

You might find this exercise really easy or you might struggle with visualization. Let your experience be your experience without judgment. But whatever happens, your perspective was different, even if only for a split second.

This exercise shows just how easy it is to change how you view the world. You might like to do it on a regular basis as a reminder that everything is an illusion interpreted through your own personal filter.

Practice gratitude

We've discussed the importance of gratitude before, but it is *such* a vital part of a Stoic lifestyle that it bears repeating.

Find ways of appreciating everything that happens to you and everyone you meet. You might like to say *thank you* in your mind at regular intervals during the day. I like to thank money every time I buy something because I appreciate being able to afford the things I need. You might like to silently thank every person you meet because their interaction taught you something new about the world.

Regularly saying thank you helps you to start seeing the world in a different way, which enables you to see opportunities everywhere and understand that there is no good or bad. There just is.

Let go of anger and fear

Notice the way you feel and if you find yourself feeling a so-called 'negative' emotion, take a moment to breathe into it. Where do you feel anger in your body? How does fear manifest? Let yourself fully embrace that emotion for a moment, then let it go. Focus your conscious mind on an emotion you feel to be the opposite and let that fill you before you respond to events around you.

If you feel afraid, focus on feeing courageous. If you feel angry, allow yourself to feel love towards the cause of that anger.

The more you observe your emotions, the more aware you become of your instinctive response and where you need to reprogram yourself in a more Stoic fashion. You will be able to identify potential opportunities everywhere and experience more peace and harmony in your life.

Make friends with difficult people

We all have people we struggle to connect with, or with whom we feel we can never get along. Actively seek out those people in your life and make the effort to befriend them. It's incredible how much seeing every single person as a possible friend will change how you interact with the people around you.

When we don't like someone, it is difficult to hide, and this disdain colors every interaction. This can be particularly problematic in the workplace and can rapidly go downhill.

Following on from the previous exercise, if you can replace the way you feel about that person with more positive emotions such as love or compassion, the way you treat them will change, which will in turn improve your relationship. Even the most difficult person has plenty to offer and can change your life for the better, no matter what your opinion might currently be.

Enjoy the freedom of creativity with your problems

Once you sit down and really consider a particular problem you're facing with an objective approach, you'll begin to realize that you have more options than you think. Some of them might be completely impractical; some of them might be highly unappealing, but just because you don't like an option or you don't think it's possible doesn't mean that it doesn't exist.

Choose a specific obstacle you are currently dealing with. Make a list of all the options available to you. Don't put any limits on yourself, just let your imagination flow. This is the time to switch off your inner censor and enjoy being creative. You might even find you enjoy this exercise because you move away from worrying about the problem and instead focus on all the opportunities it can open up for you.

Once you have your list of potential actions, go through each one by turn and list out the possible outcomes if you choose that route. If you cannot think of many, at the very least, note the best- and worst-case scenarios. Try to be honest. Set your emotions aside for now. Don't have any attachment to a particular course of action because you may well find that something else occurs to you that is a much better choice.

Once you are done, you should have a clear picture of where you will go once you've chosen the best action. This is your way forward.

Figure out your purpose

Some people can spend their whole lives trying and failing to find their true purpose. This process may take you years, but the more you actively strive to follow your path, the more you find you are doing exactly what you are 'supposed' to, even if you can't actively explain your purpose to others.

Start by making a list of all the things that light you up. What brings you joy? What would you spend your time doing if money weren't an option? What did you want to be when you were a child? What did you choose to do when you were little? What did you use to love but have somehow let fall away even though you'd still enjoy doing it? Include on your list things you think you'd like but haven't been able to do for whatever reason.

Once you have your list, review it for common themes. Why do/ did you like those things so much? What new things would you like to try? Do you still love the things you liked when you were a child? Why? Why not?

Go through your list and do everything on it. If you said you liked reading, set aside a whole day to catch up on all the books sitting on your Kindle that you haven't found the time to start. If you enjoyed dancing, put on some music and boogie away. Do every single thing for as long as you feel you need to discover how you feel about it. Journal how you feel about all of your thoughts and feelings about each activity while you were doing it and after you finished. This is for your eyes only, so don't worry about hurting anyone's feelings. Write out everything, the good and the bad, so you get a full picture of what inspires you and fills you with positivity.

Now make a list of all of your strengths. What are you good at doing? What do other people tell you you are good at doing? Why? Dig deep. "Just because" is not a good enough answer.

Once you have this list, ask yourself how much you love doing these things. You might be good at doing something, but if it doesn't excite you, it's not going to be your purpose.

If it is not something you can see yourself doing every day and still love it for the rest of your life, it's not part of your true path.

You can repeat this exercise with all aspects of your life. You might find it helpful to list out the people you admire and respect and look at all the qualities that speak to you. What kind of person are you drawn to? Who would you like to be like? Who would you hate to be like?

This deep introspection may take you weeks, if not months, and that's okay. This is a journey, not a destination, and it's important that you really get to know yourself and your motivations. Once you are done, look back over your journal and reflect on what you've learned. You might even want to repeat it to focus on the things with which you felt a stronger connection.

The more you do this, the more you'll get a sense of what you love. The best bit is that you will have had a lot of fun experimenting while you explore yourself. You'll naturally find yourself gravitating to things that make you happy and you'll be struck by random bursts of inspiration. For example, you might discover that you love gardening and give up your office job to become a landscape gardener. Instantly, your mood lifts because you're so much happier at work and you start to attract more of the kind of people you want to be around.

This exercise might take a long time, but every moment you spend working through it takes you closer and closer towards the life you were meant to live.

Summary

The secret to living like Marcus Aurelius is to take a negative and transform it into a positive.

- Shift your perspective. Something is 'good' or 'bad' because that is the value judgment we have made.
- Be grateful for everything. This is a key aspect of living a Stoic life.
- Actively choose to release negative emotions such as anger or fear.
- Try to befriend difficult people instead of seeking conflict with them.
- Be creative in how you approach problem solving. The chances are high you have more options open to you than you initially think.
- Find your life's true path and then follow it. The worst that can happen is that you have some fun while you're figuring out where to go!

PART THREE:

SENECA

THE LIFE OF SENECA

As is a tale, so is life: not how long it is,
but how good it is, is what matters.

—Seneca

Lucius Annaeus Seneca the Younger was born c. 4BC in Corduba, a Roman province in Hispania. He was the middle of three brothers. His father, Lucius Annaeus Seneca the Elder, was a writer and teacher of rhetoric, and his mother, Helvia, came from a wealthy, influential Baetician family.

Very little is truly known about Seneca's life before he was sent into exile in 41AD, although that hasn't prevented some historians from speculating about what might have happened in those years (for which we have no surviving evidence).

According to Seneca's own writing, he was taken to Rome in the 'arms' of his mother's stepsister at an early age, probably when he was around five years old. His father was well established in the city, where he lived for most of his life. As was common with high-born Romans, Seneca studied literature, grammar, and rhetoric. He also studied philosophy under Attalus the Stoic, so was familiar with the school of thought from a young age. Other teachers included Sotion and Papirius Fabianus, who were members of the short-lived School of the Sextii, which blended Stoicism with Pythagorean thought.

Under Sotion's influence, Seneca became a vegetarian in his early twenties, a lifestyle he practiced for roughly a year before his father persuaded him to return to eating meat because he associated vegetarianism with "some foreign rites."

Seneca suffered from various health issues, including breathing difficulties, which are now believed to be asthma. He became seriously ill in his mid-twenties with what was most likely tuberculosis. He went to Egypt to recover, where he stayed with the same aunt who had taken him to Rome when he was younger. She nursed him through his sickness, the healing process taking as long as ten years before he was fully recovered.

In 31AD, Seneca and his aunt returned to Rome, but his uncle died on the journey following a shipwreck. His aunt's influence played a major role in the election of Seneca to quaestor, which meant that he was entitled to a place in the Roman Senate.

By all accounts, Seneca's early years as a senator were successful, with him being singled out for especial praise for his oratory. In fact, according to Cassius Dio, Seneca was so skilled a public speaker that Caligula was offended and ordered that the senator kill himself. Seneca was only able to evade the order because he was seriously ill at the time and Caligula was informed that he was going to die soon regardless. Perhaps because of this attempt at ending his life, Seneca had nothing positive to say about Caligula in his notes, recording his worst traits and behaviors.

Seneca was not the only one to believe the emperor was a monster. In 41AD, Caligula was assassinated by a mob and Claudius became emperor. However, the new regime was not the end of Seneca's problem with authority. He was accused by the new empress, Messalina, of committing adultery with Julia Livilla, Caligula and Agrippina's sister. Many historians doubt the veracity of this claim, as there were obvious political motives for Messalina wanting to remove

Julia Livilla and her supporters. Nevertheless, the Senate sentenced Seneca to death, a sentence that was commuted to exile by Claudius. As a consequence, Seneca spent eight years living as an exile on the island of Corsica.

Two of Seneca's earliest surviving texts were written during his exile, both consolations. *Consolation to Helvia* was written for his mother and sees Seneca offering comfort for her loss, as he was effectively out of her life. In this work, Seneca discusses the death of his own son, which had occurred not long before his exile. It is unclear who the mother of his child was. While Seneca was later married to Pompeia Paulina, some believe that he had his son with a previous wife, but there is little evidence to support this theory.

Seneca's second surviving work from this time is *Consolation to Polybius,* which surrounds the death of Polybius' brother. In this text, Seneca speaks highly of Claudius and states that he hopes that the emperor will recall him from exile at some point. This is indeed what happened when Agrippina married Claudius (who also happened to be her uncle) in 49AD. She was able to influence the emperor to recall Seneca to Rome. Once there, Agrippina was able to use her connections to grant praetorship to Seneca. She also appointed him to tutor her son, a young man who would one day become the emperor Nero.

Seneca served as Nero's advisor from 54-62AD alongside praetorian prefect Sextus Afranius Burrus. As a result of this position, Seneca was appointed suffect consul in 56AD.

During his first year of working for the emperor, Seneca was able to have a major influence on the new ruler. He was the one who wrote Nero's accession speeches, promising to return all proper legal procedures and authorities to the Senate. He was also behind Nero's eulogy for Claudius, which he gave at the funeral.

In addition, sometime during these early years of Nero's reign, Seneca wrote a satirical piece, *Apocolocyntosis*, which mocked the deification of Claudius and spoke of Nero's positive qualities. In 55AD, Seneca penned *On Clemency*. Written in response to Nero's murder of Britannicus, it is possible that he was hoping to reassure people that this was the last time they would see the emperor engage in such violence. While the piece shows Nero in a possible light, it also details a very Stoic approach to being a virtuous leader.

Contemporary observers such as Tacitus and Dio appear to agree that during the early years of Nero's rule, when Seneca's influence was at its height, the emperor was not bad at fulfilling his duties. However, over time, Seneca's ability to affect the emperor's decisions waned as he descended into madness and cruelty. In 59AD, Seneca was forced into supporting Agrippina's murder, and Tacitus wrote about how Seneca had to pen a letter to the Senate explaining why the murder was essential

Seneca himself was subject to personal attacks. In 58AD, senator Publius Suilius Rufus made a number of public accusations that were very damaging to him. According to Tacitus and Dio, Suilius accused Seneca of having built up a huge fortune during the first four years of Nero's rule. Allegedly he had made three hundred million sestertii through charging high interest on loans. Suilius also accused Seneca of having an affair with Agrippina, a very serious charge. However, Tacitus countered these allegations by pointing out that Suilius had reason to want to undermine Seneca. He had been close to Claudius and had himself embezzled and passed on information.

Seneca's reaction to the accusations was to respond in kind. He brought a number of prosecutions for corruption against his rival, who had half of his estate confiscated before being sent into exile.

However, Suilius was hardly the only person to openly take issue with Seneca, who had to deal with similar attacks throughout his career. Seneca was a wealthy man with properties in numerous locations throughout the Roman empire, as well as in Egypt. Dio even blames the Boudica uprising in Britannia on Seneca, claiming that he had forced the indigenous British aristocracy into taking out loans only to call them in without warning, aggressively enforcing repayments.

Despite his Stoic beliefs, Seneca was not above defending himself against these accusations. In his *De Vita Beata* ("On the Happy Life"), which was written during this period, Seneca argues that acquiring property and enjoying all the privileges of wealth were completely appropriate for a Stoic philosopher.

Seneca had been working alongside Burrus, but after his colleague died in 62AD, Seneca's influence quickly fell away. Seneca attempted to retire in 62 and 64AD, but Nero wouldn't let him. Instead, Seneca spent more and more time away from court, choosing to spend time in his country estates studying and writing and avoiding Rome as much as possible. This period saw him write two of his greatest works, *Naturales Quaestoines,* a collection of facts about the natural world, and *Letters to Lucilius,* which explores his philosophical musings.

In 65AD, there had been a plot to assassinate Nero. Seneca became associated with the conspiracy, and while it is unlikely he had anything to do with the plot, he was caught up in the aftermath and ordered to commit suicide by Nero.

As was tradition at the time, Seneca cut a number of veins so that he could bleed to death, his wife doing the same. According to Dio, Seneca had attempted to finish writing a few last-minute letters, so the soldiers intervened to make sure he died quickly. In comparison, Tacitus stated that Nero had ordered that Seneca's wife be spared, so the soldiers bound her wounds and she did not try again to kill herself.

Seneca's death was not quick. His advanced age and diet were blamed for his blood flowing slowly, causing him to suffer for longer than should have been necessary. As such, he also took poison, which also failed to kill him. In the end, Seneca dictated his final words to a scribe and then, surrounded by friends, climbed into a warm bath to speed up the flow of blood and provide some pain relief. Tacitus stated, "He was then carried into a bath, with the steam of which he was suffocated, and he was burnt without any of the usual funeral rites. So he had directed in a codicil of his will, even when in the height of his wealth and power he was thinking of life's close." Some would argue that Seneca had demonstrated the ultimately Stoic approach to death, while at the same time there were others who felt that his behavior had been histrionic and unnecessarily performative, the very opposite of Stoicism.

Seneca has been described as one of the leading philosophical figures of the Roman Imperial Period and he played a major role in the development of Stoicism. His work is easy to understand and as a consequence had a big influence on later philosophers, most notably from the Renaissance onwards.

He wrote many books about Stoicism with a large focus on ethics. He expanded on the work of earlier Stoics, particularly singling out Zeno, Cleanthes, and Chrysippus as having had an influence on him. In addition, he often quoted Epicurus for his views on ethics.

Stoicism shines through all of Seneca's work. It was a popular philosophy of the time with many upper-class Romans turning to it for guidance. His writing looks at both theory and practice, with his opinion being that they were distinct but interdependent. He viewed philosophy as being the way to cope with the pressures of life. He felt that those negative emotions such as anger and grief should be eliminated or at least moderated. He also believed that it was important to confront your own mortality in order to be able to face death, a viewpoint that is exemplified in how he handled his own passing.

Ultimately, Seneca's attitude was that it was best to approach life calmly, rationally, and objectively, balancing whatever happened with an understanding and acceptance that adversity is simply part of life.

MEMENTO MORI

*You want to live but do you know how to live? You are scared
of dying and tell me, is the kind of life you lead really any
different from being dead?*

—Seneca

Seneca's Stoic approach to life no doubt sustained him when it came to his death, and there is one particular concept which would have been of particular comfort: *Memento Mori.* This process involves considering your own mortality. After all, death is the only certainty yet so many of us, particularly in the Western world, spend our lives trying to avoid thinking about it or dealing with it.

Memento Mori is a practice even older than Stoicism. According to Socrates, the whole purpose of philosophy was to consider "dying and being dead." The Stoics built upon this notion to incorporate it into their practical philosophy, which enabled them to appreciate life all the more.

The simple reality is that we can all die at any time. You could cross the road tomorrow and be hit by a bus, eat contaminated shellfish and suffer food poisoning, or be one of the four people a year who die while putting on their trousers. Because death can come when you least expect it, you should use that fact to guide everything you do, say, or think. You really should live each day as if it's your last. Do not wait to start living a virtuous life. Don't tell yourself that you'll do what makes you happy one day when circumstances are perfect. Things will never be perfect and there's never an excuse to delay today because tomorrow may not happen for you.

To some people, the notion of focusing on their own demise is a depressing thought, but if that's your response, you've missed the whole point of this exercise. To a Stoic, considering dying serves as an inspiration, reminding us that we are all mere mortals. Seneca said that when you retire for the night, you should remind yourself that 'you may not wake up tomorrow' and then when you awake, tell yourself that 'you may not sleep again.'

When you are constantly aware that life is fleeting, it becomes a motivator to make the most of whatever time is remaining to you. Be your best self at all times. Many of us have experienced this feeling when we have lost someone dear to us or had an experience which has shaken us, such as a car accident or illness, because we have come close to losing our life. But over time, the power of that experience wanes and it becomes difficult to maintain the same attitude.

Conversely, some find the thought of dying so frightening that it holds them back from living to their full potential, locking themselves away and hiding from anything perceived as dangerous.

The secret to living like Seneca is to remember that if you have done your best to live a meaningful life, there is no need to be afraid of death. It is a natural part of life and comes to us all. Because you cannot evade death, doesn't it make sense to prepare yourself for it, whenever it may happen, by living a life filled with purpose and virtue?

Many of us have an idea of what we would love to do if we knew we only had a short time left. If you knew it was your last day on earth, you probably wouldn't work. You might like to spend time with your loved ones to build a final few memories with them and forget about all the bills you've still got to pay or that major deadline looming at work. You might do something that breaks societal taboos like try drugs for the first time or have an affair because you'll be dead before you have to deal with the consequences of your behavior.

The problem is that if you're not actually dying, you've then got to live with the consequences of your actions, which is why we don't throw caution to the wind and act as though we're in our final few hours of life. And of course, this isn't what the Stoics were advising when it came to practicing *Memento Mori.*

When you live every day as if it's your last, it means asking yourself, *Have I always been my best self? Have I been kind and compassionate towards everyone I've encountered? Have I truly given my best at work? In my relationships? In my friendships?*

If I died right now, what would be my legacy?

When you consider death in this manner, it loses its hold over you and inspires you to do your best on even the most mundane of days. When you journal at night, you can reflect on whether you'd made time for the people who are important to you or if you'd allowed yourself to be distracted by social media and keeping up appearances to people who simply don't matter. You can consider the choices you've made that day and whether they were the most virtuous. You can decide whether you really had the best possible day or if you could have done more to be a better person – and then improve tomorrow.

Exercises

Journal about death

We've already discussed the value of incorporating journaling into your daily life. You should incorporate Memento Mori into your journaling, ideally every day, but even if you only consider your mortality once a week it is still a valuable exercise.

You might like to use these prompts as a framework:

1. Make a list of all the people you dealt with that day. If you deal with a lot of people online for whatever reason, you might like to limit this solely to people you encountered in real life or prioritize the most important ones.

2. Consider your interactions with them. Were you your best self? Is there anything you could have done to improve things? Do you need to apologize for your behavior or forgive them for theirs?

3. Make a list of all the reasons you're grateful for your interaction with them. Did you learn anything? Do you now have treasured memories?

4. Explore the notion that today has been your last day. Are you satisfied with how it went? Was it the legacy you would like to leave the world?

Practice forgiveness

Forgiveness doesn't mean that you have to forget or excuse someone hurting you. Nor does it mean that you have to allow someone back into your life if you have established healthy boundaries that involve no longer having contact with them. It certainly doesn't mean that you have to open yourself up to being hurt again or repeating past mistakes.

However, forgiveness brings with it so many benefits. When you can finally let go of how someone has harmed you, even unintentionally, it allows us to fully heal. We can reprogram those stories which have arisen from past hurts, such as *I don't deserve love* or *I can never be suc-*

cessful, because we have released the hold they have over us. Forgiveness can improve your self-esteem and help you feel whole and safe.

There are many ways you can forgive someone. You might like to put together a little forgiveness ritual, writing out the ways someone has hurt you and then burning the paper to release any associated feelings. You can hold thoughts of the person you need to forgive in your mind while chanting to yourself *I forgive you* over and over until you feel that you have moved on.

Remember to forgive yourself too. There may be part of you that holds yourself accountable for what happened. Forgiving yourself brings with it a sense of freedom, which is genuinely liberating.

Plan your own funeral

Many of us have no idea about the events and emotions at the end of life until we have to deal with the death of a loved one. We have no idea about all our options when it comes to arranging a funeral so default to our nearest funeral home and let them handle all the details.

This is understandable. When we are in the immediacy of fresh grief, the last thing we want to do is shop around or learn about how to wrap a body in a shroud.

Planning your own funeral serves so many purposes. Not only does it force you to consider your own mortality, you remove the stress from your family of having to plan things when they would be better off focusing on emotionally supporting each other, as well as guaranteeing that your funeral really does reflect your final wishes. When you have arranged everything yourself, your friends and family have the reassurance of knowing that the funeral reflects who you truly were.

Exploring your options opens up a world of possibilities. For example, did you know that you don't have to use a funeral home at all? And that you can keep a body in your own home until the funeral? You can use a shroud instead of a coffin. Choose a green burial instead of burial in a churchyard.

There are so many choices you may not be aware of and if money is a concern, you'll soon discover that a funeral really doesn't have to cost the thousands most people spend.

One of the most important aspects of a funeral is the eulogy and you should take time to write an *honest* eulogy about yourself. Unlike someone writing about you, you are under no obligation to gloss over the negative, so consider what people would say if they weren't bound by social convention. Would your children say you spent enough time with them? Would your partner talk about what a loving, considerate person you were? Would your friends say that they admired you for the person you were because you always strived to live a good life?

Or would they say you could have done so much more?

It doesn't matter if your eulogy shows that you could have been a better person. Unlike the real thing, you have plenty of time to write a new one. Start changing your behavior to reflect the person you would like to be and come back to your eulogy on a regular basis to see how your legacy can change.

Treat your life as an opportunity to write the perfect eulogy.

Tell your family and friends how much you love them

Many of us hold back from expressing how we truly feel about the people around us. You should never be afraid to tell those you care about how much they matter to you. Love unconditionally. As a Stoic, you understand that you only have control over yourself, so you shouldn't love someone based on how they feel about you. You can't make someone love you.

So love freely and don't worry about whether it comes back to you from a particular person. The important thing is that people know how you felt about them when it's your time to die.

Read books about death and dying

One of the best ways to learn about how death impacts people is to study the subject in great depth. There are countless excellent books and memoirs on the subject that let you see how others have dealt with death and what the experience taught them.

Go to your local library or browse bookshops or Amazon to find books that will inspire you.

Here are some ideas to get you started:

- *The Conversation* by Angelo Volandes
- *Knocking on Heaven's Door* by Katy Butler
- *The Year of Magical Thinking* by Joan Didion
- *The Best Care Possible: A Physician's Quest to Transform Care Through the End of Life* by Ira Byock
- *Can't We Talk About Something More Pleasant* by Roz Chast
- *On Death and Dying* by Elisabeth Kübler-Ross
- *Being Mortal by* Atul Gawande
- *The Shift: One Nurse, Twelve Hours, Four Patients' Lives* by Therese Brown
- *The Fault in our Stars* by John Green
- *How We Die: Reflections of Life's Final Chapter* by Sherwin B. Nuland
- *When Breath Becomes Air* by Paul Kalanithi
- *Nothing to be Frightened of* by Julian Barnes
- *The Bright Hour: A Memoir of Living and Dying* by Nina Riggs
- *The End of your Life Book Club* by Will Schwalbe
- *Dying: A Memoir* by Cory Taylor

Meditate on death

Spend some time meditating on mortality, both yours and those around you.

Think about someone you love, someone you couldn't bear to be without. Imagine that they've just died. How do you feel when you first get the news? What would be your immediate reaction? What would you do without them in your life? Would you cope or would you struggle?

If you find yourself crying, this is okay. Let it all out. Really put yourself in the moment and allow yourself to experience the loss as if it were actually happening. You will find that the more you do this, the more you appreciate that person in your life and become inspired to be your best self around them.

You should also set aside time to meditate on your own mortality.

Find a time and place where you will not be disturbed for a few minutes. Sit quietly, close your eyes, and turn your attention to your breath. Observe its flow for a few moments. Do not attempt to control it in any way. Simply allow it to flow, nurturing your body, mind, and soul.

When you are ready, ask yourself: *Do I agree that death is inevitable?* See what answers come to you. If you don't get anything, this is absolutely fine. Let your experience be your experience. Ask yourself the same question again, and then one final time.

Next, ask yourself: *If I died today, can I say I lived my best life?* Let whatever answers arise as they will before asking yourself the same question two more times.

Finally, ask yourself: *Can I live today/tomorrow as if it were my last day?* Adapt the question according to whether you are meditating in the morning or evening. Again, allow answers to come to you without judgment. Ask the question two more times.

Finally, imagine that you have died and you are able to observe your funeral. How are people feeling about your passing? What are they saying about you? Try to be honest here rather than imagining how you would like people to act.

Ask yourself one last question: *What can I do to improve myself to change how people would mourn me?*

Sit with your thoughts for a little while and when you are ready, open your eyes. I would advise recording your thoughts and observations in your journal so that you can see how your attitudes change over time.

Summary

The secret to living like Seneca is to remember that if you have done your best to live a meaningful life – there is no need to be afraid of death. It is a natural part of life and comes to us all.

- Journal about death. You can use the prompts in this book or use some of your own.
- Practice forgiveness.
- Plan your own funeral, including writing your eulogy. Not only is this a valuable exercise, but it will also help alleviate some of the stress on your loved ones when you do pass.
- Don't be afraid to tell your family and friends how much you love them.
- Familiarize yourself with death by reading books about death and dying.
- Meditate on death.

VALUE THE TIME YOU HAVE - WHICH IS MORE THAN ENOUGH

Hang on to your youthful enthusiasms — you'll be able to use them better when you're older.

—Seneca

Having just spent a chapter focusing on death and how life is short, it may be surprising to hear that the Stoics believed that we all are given plenty of time to do what is truly important. In Seneca's essay, *De Brevitate Vitae* (On the Shortness of Life), he argues that we should all make the best use of however much time we are given on earth because there is always enough to do what is important.

The secret to living like Seneca is to spend your time living a virtuous life.

He wrote "It is not that we have so little time but that we lose so much. ... The life we receive is not short but we make it so; we are not ill provided but use what we have wastefully." This time is wasted because we are not living in the now. Instead, we are worried about the future and stressing about the past, allowing the present to slip through our fingers. Yet if we don't make the most of what is happening right this second, we've lost the only thing we ever really have: this moment.

Seneca held that the reason we waste time is because we do not place the same level of value on it as we do money or our possessions, despite the fact that it is the one thing we cannot get more of. We are born with an allotted span and no amount of effort will change that. In comparison, it is always possible to earn more money or buy more things.

Time is intangible. We cannot see it or hold it. As such, most people struggle to place a value on it, giving it away to anyone because it doesn't have any worth for us. A Stoic understands that time is the only thing we have, which makes it the most precious thing there is. When you accept this truth, it becomes easier to stay in the present moment. You cannot go back in time to change the past. You cannot force the future to be what you want it to be. All you can do is shape the now and find happiness in whatever is currently occurring.

We will explore the notion of mindfulness in greater depth in the next chapter, but it is important to mention it here because the practice is a crucial part of making the most of your time. When you decide to be completely aware of all that you do and focus on your thoughts and actions as they occur, you allow yourself to be open to any possibility. Studies have shown that mindfulness can make you more creative, more compassionate, and better grounded in the world.

While a Stoic mindset encourages you to release any attachment to material things or making value judgments about 'good' or 'bad' experiences, that does not mean that you become some sort of emotionless automaton. You are allowed to have possessions that bring you pleasure – the ancient Stoics certainly did! You are allowed to be sad when something negative occurs. It's just that you are focusing more on being your best self instead of stressing about status and accepting that life is filled with ups and downs, which is just the way it is.

The Stoics understood that the pursuit of material wealth was a distraction. The only thing worth seeking was virtue. Be wise, just, brave, and self-aware. When you embody your highest self, *that's* when you are truly rich. Anything else is a bonus.

One important teaching of Stoicism is the concept of universal citizenship. We might feel that we are not making a big difference in our daily life, but every step we take on a virtuous path has a ripple effect, making society that little bit better. If everyone focused on living a virtuous life, then the world would be a beautiful, harmonious place.

When you sit back and look at all the issues facing the world today, it can feel overwhelming. What can any of us do to combat climate change, societal inequalities, or animal abuse? Quite a lot, as it happens. You always have a choice over which businesses you give your money to. You can buy local or direct from suppliers instead of going to large stores or shopping with big businesses like Amazon. You have a choice over the kind of food you buy, so can be vegetarian or vegan or decide to only consume meat from ethical farmers who give their animals a good quality of life. You have a choice over the kind of car you drive or may decide not to drive at all. You have a choice over the clothes you buy, so you can upcycle second-hand clothes, shop only in charity or vintage stores, or buy your clothes from ethical companies that don't use sweatshops.

Every single time you spend your money, you are making a choice that shapes the world in some small way, whether you are aware of it or not. If you have been buying things without considering how they are sourced and how they get into your hands, as a Stoic, you need to start being more intentional in your spending habits. As Seneca puts it, "Until we have begun to go without them, we fail to realize how unnecessary many things are. We've been using them not because we needed them but because we had them."

This is all part of living a more virtuous life – if you are buying things for the sake of it, or aren't actively choosing to support ethical suppliers, you are undermining your efforts to be virtuous. Not only that, you are also negatively impacting the world at large, putting pressure on the world and forcing others to work in poor conditions just so you can purchase something. Is it really worth it?

I want to make an important point here: Stoicism is a philosophy with no religious or political affiliation. As such, it is not anti-capitalist. What it actually *is* is pragmatic and practical. Two people can look at all the evidence for a particular political standpoint and come to completely different conclusions, both equally valid. There is no political leaning to reason, so it is up to you as a Stoic to come to your own conclusions over the best way forward in any given situation, having weighed the evidence. You have a duty to act against immorality and inequality in whatever way seems most logical to you. You get to define your own personal path and decide what virtue looks like to you.

It takes courage to stand up and fight injustice when you see it. It takes bravery to make a stand against societal norms when they cause inequality. As a Stoic, it is your responsibility to develop that courage so that you can do your part in creating a fairer, more equitable society.

It is the virtuous thing to do.

Exercises

Be more intentional in your spending

Whether we like to acknowledge it or not, the existence of humans on this planet will always cause at least some harm. It is impossible to eliminate the damage you are doing just by living. When you travel, you are damaging the environment, even if you are walking. You might step on an insect, for example, and the more people who travel over a particular ground, the more it gets worn away. When you buy food to eat, it has a carbon footprint. It is difficult to know how the people who gathered and packaged it were treated.

When you start thinking about all the different ways you are harming society and the planet just by being you, it can be overwhelming. Take comfort in knowing that this is simply the way of things, but you can minimize the damage you do, which is the Stoic thing to do.

As a Stoic, you should seek to become a more conscious consumer. Sometimes you have to make a judgment call and that's okay. You might want to buy nothing but organic products, but if it's simply too expensive, it is fine to shop within your means. We are all flawed. As long as you do your best, it's good enough.

Start by tracking your spending. Make a note of everything you buy for a month so you can get a sense of where you should be focusing your attention.

Once you have an idea of your shopping habits, you can put together a personalized action plan to improve things. Are you spending money on things you don't need? Think about how you can cut back. If you are comfort shopping, there may well be underlying reasons, so you might even want to consider seeking professional help to deal with those impulses.

Look at **where** you've spent money. Can you change where you shop? Are there ethical businesses you can support?

Start looking at where your food comes from. Try to buy food that has been sourced locally or shop directly from farm shops if that is an option for you. Eating food in season also helps you to keep your environmental impact low.

What brand toiletries do you buy? Are you purchasing from companies that are truly ethical? There are many websites that can tell you the truth about the products you buy. You can choose to buy biodegradable products or those that do not contain palm oil.

This might seem a mammoth task, but all you have to do is start small. Select **one** thing to change and do it until it becomes habit. Then move on to something else. Every little step you take is further along the path to virtuousness.

Donate your time to charities

As we've discussed, time is the most valuable thing in our possession. While charities need money to keep going, it is very easy to throw cash at a charity and think that you've done your part. Yet that probably isn't the most virtuous things to do. Many large charities are not ethical in their spending and do not use that money in a way that best supports their purposes. Your money may not be helping those you intended to support.

Small local charities are always in need of volunteers and when you help them out, it gives you a different perspective on the world. You'll also be able to see the difference your work makes and know that you really have made a change.

Even if there isn't a charity you would like to work with, there are always things you can do to improve your little corner of the world.

You can pick up trash in your area or ask an elderly neighbor if there's anything you can do to help them.

There are always ways of spending your time in a virtuous manner to improve the world in some small way.

Summary

The secret to living like Seneca is to spend your time living a virtuous life.

- Become more intentional in your consumerism in whatever way makes sense to you.
- Spend time helping out charities rather than donating money.

MINDFULNESS THE STOIC WAY

He suffers more than necessary, who suffers before it is necessary.
—Seneca

In this chapter we're going to dig deep into the notion of mindfulness. Mindfulness is becoming increasingly popular for those seeking relief from the stress of modern living. Put simply, it involves focusing all your attention on the present moment, releasing any concern or attachment to the past or future. After all, this is the only thing any of us can have, and while the Stoics may not have called what they did mindfulness, it's exactly what they were practising.

As you know by now, your ultimate aim as a Stoic is to live a virtuous life. In order for you to fully embrace this, your mind should always be directed towards taking a moderate, self-aware approach to whatever happens. This constant focus might sound like it would be impossible to maintain but remember – you are walking the path to virtuousness. It's okay to stumble along the way or take detours on occasion. All you can ever do is your best.

However, if you set an intention to be fully mindful in your thoughts and actions, you'll gradually find you get better and better at what you do.

It's all about remembering what you can control and only working on that. And what's the only thing you can control? That's right. Yourself.

The more you remember that you have control over what you do and think, the easier it becomes to be mindful. Sometimes you might find yourself caught up in an emotional response. Once you are aware of what's going on, you can pause to ask yourself whether this is the best reaction to a situation. Are you letting the things outside your control take away your time and energy? As soon as you realize what's going on, you can take steps to be more mindful. It's never too late to change how you are handling a situation, even when you are caught up in the middle of a storm.

When you are mindful in your thoughts and behavior, one beneficial side effect is that you become increasingly self-aware. Let's say that you are faced with choosing what subjects to study at college. You know that if you choose law, you will be fulfilling your parents' aspirations for you, but if you choose art, they will feel you are wasting your potential and worry that you will never be able to make a comfortable living.

It is natural to follow a path that will make your parents happy, but as a Stoic, you should understand that their happiness is not within your power. *They* choose how they feel, just as you do. All you can do is be your best self and make those choices that take you down the path to virtue.

You might decide, having carefully considered the results of your actions, that you will study law but take a night class in art. Naturally, this will make your parents happy, but that is not the motive behind your choice. What *is* important to you is your earning potential, whether you will be fulfilled by your studies, how hard you are willing to work to get good grades, and how you can express your artistic side. These are all within your control and things you can change. Your parents' emotions don't come into the equation.

If you find yourself placing the opinions of others above your own, you will never be able to fully embody your best self. If you can keep your focus only on those things you can control, not only do you free yourself from societal expectations, you'll also find that life becomes more fulfilling and you are more motivated to continue along your Stoic path.

There is one potential problem with focusing on yourself that you should be aware of so that you can take steps to avoid it: if you allow your ego to get in the way, you may find yourself becoming selfish and not taking into account how you are impacting others. After all, the only thing they can control are *their* thoughts and feelings, so it's their choice to be upset by your behavior and has nothing to do with you.

If this is your attitude, you have missed the point. The Stoics worked with the goal of virtue in mind. As a Stoic, you are aiming to live a virtuous life with the goal of not just being a better person but building a better society for all. So, with every choice, you can decide to do whatever is of most benefit to all. Going back to the example of choosing what subject to study, you might pursue art, not because it will upset your parents, but because you've done your research, have a strong vision of what you want to do in your artistic career, and have the self-awareness to know that if you were to do law, you would likely fail, as it's not a passion. Then, when you become a successful artist, your parents are likely to be happy for you because they will understand the decisions you made. But if they aren't, you have done your best, which is all you can do.

According to the Stoics, you can only live a virtuous life when you place your attention on what is under your control *and* always strive towards being a good person. If you are worried about what's going on around you or what might happen, you give away your power and suffer. If you only care about your own happiness and don't consider the impact you have on those around you, you will never be your best self.

The secret to living like Seneca is to be mindful about your motives, thoughts, feelings, and actions so that you can choose to be the most virtuous person possible.

The ancient Stoics were inspired by nature and firmly believed that it had designed mankind to live in harmony with one another and the world around them. They felt that when you follow your natural inclinations, everyone would treat one another with kindness and compassion. We would do the right thing because it is the right thing, rather than because we care about showing others what a nice person we are.

The mindful way of being Stoic is more than just living in the moment, which is an important principle. Stoics built on this to ensure that they were always being virtuous by keeping their attention on what they could control and allowing themselves to be ruled by practising kindness towards those around them.

The Stoics believed in the 'community of humankind' and thus lived with an aim of creating a better world for all.

Exercises

Just breathe

There is a reason why you are advised to just breathe when you are angry. The act of breathing is incredibly powerful and is one of the simplest forms of mindfulness.

If you find yourself becoming emotional or overwhelmed, turn your attention to your breath, even if only for a couple of inhalation and exhalations. Close your eyes and focus on the breath as it flows in and out of your body. Let it bring you back to the present moment and once you are there, move forward with the choices your best self would make.

Respond with love

It can be difficult to respond with kindness when someone does something to annoy us. Even small actions that really don't matter in the grand scheme of things can quickly spiral out of control if we let them.

While it might feel difficult, when someone upsets you, you should respond with love. Remember that we are all part of the community of humankind and thus are all connected. This does not mean that you should allow someone to walk all over you – it is okay to remove yourself from a situation if it becomes unbearable or stand up for yourself when you are being attacked. But rather than meeting aggression with aggression, take the opposite approach. The more someone yells at you, the quieter and more reasonable your voice should become. It's amazing how quickly you can defuse a situation simply by responding to anger with a calm, measured reaction.

You can use your journal to support this process. When you have been in a difficult situation, write about what you did and what you could have done instead. Explore the various motivations for the person you were in conflict with. When you have listed out all their possible motives, choose the kindest one to explain their position. When you look at this, does it make it easier to come from a place of love the next time you are in a similar situation?

Regularly practice the Compassion Prayer

You may have heard of the loving kindness meditation, or metta meditation, but there is another practice that also makes it easier to respond with love no matter what happens. The Compassion Prayer is another form of meditation that supports you to be kinder and more compassionate to the people around you.

Make yourself comfortable, close your eyes, and turn your attention to your breath. Spend a few moments fully focused on the air flowing in and out of your body, keeping you in this moment.

When you feel calm, relaxed, and present, bring to mind someone with whom you have a strong connection. This might be someone whom you have recently been in conflict with, but if the emotions are still too raw for you to send kindness to yourself, it is absolutely fine to use someone you feel more positively about. As your practice of this meditation continues, you will find it easier to aim it at anyone, but when you are starting out, it is absolutely fine to practice kindness to yourself first and work with someone with whom you can do this exercise and not get more upset or feel hypocritical.

Once you have thought of your person, start to send good things to them. Say to yourself phrases such as *I wish you always feel loved, I wish you are always supported, I wish you never feel alone,* and *I wish you happiness and joy.* You can use any phrases you like as long as they are filled with positive, unconditional love. As you send these wishes to the person you have chosen, imagine yourself saying it to them in person and consider what their reaction would be. Do not censor your imagination. Just let it flow as you converse with them in your mind and send them your best wishes.

This exercise is best done daily. You can work with different people each time you do the Compassion Prayer, maybe focusing on those you have disagreed with to help you be more compassionate and loving towards them in future, or you can work with one person on a long-term basis if you feel that your relationship with them can be improved. You can just work with people you have a positive relationship with if you prefer – this is *your* practice, so you get to choose how you do it.

When you have finished your meditation, journal what happened. You might like to note how you felt towards the person before the meditation and how this has changed afterwards.

The more you do the Compassion Prayer, the more you will find yourself becoming more loving and kinder towards yourself and the people around you, making it easier to respond with love, whatever happens.

Summary

The secret to living like Seneca is to be mindful about your motives, thoughts, feelings, and actions so that you can choose to be the most virtuous person possible.

- When you feel yourself losing your control or coming out of the moment, just breathe.
- Send love to others, even when they are upsetting you.
- Practice the compassion prayer.

FINAL THOUGHTS

N
ow that you have finished this book, it should become clear that Stoicism is a practical philosophy, above all else. It is not enough to read about it; in order to fully understand it, you have to embody it in everything you say, think, and do. However, there is a *lot* of information in this book, and you may be feeling too overwhelmed to know where to start.

Just breathe.

Stoicism is a journey. It is a practice, not a perfected art. It's certainly not a race. Wherever you are on your path to a virtuous life is absolutely fine. If you pick just **one** exercise and implement it, you are already doing a great job. It is better to take small steps and keep going than attempt to run, fall flat on your face, and give up.

If you don't know where to start, personally, I would begin with journaling. This underpins so many exercises in this book and once you have established a journaling practice, you can then use your journal to observe what is and isn't working for you as you gradually bring in other Stoic behaviors and approaches.

Another good place to start is the Compassion Prayer. This will help you avoid putting too much pressure on yourself to live up to artificially high standards. It will support you to release expectations and take each moment as it comes, in true Stoic fashion.

As Marcus Aurelius wrote, "Today I escaped from anxiety. Or no, I discarded it, because it was within me, in my own perceptions — not outside."

Let today be the day you escape from **your** anxieties.

THANKS FOR READING

I hope that you enjoyed reading this book and that the practical exercises have been valuable.

If you are looking for more daily practical exercises, as well as quotes, journaling prompts, self-reflections and more, I encourage you to check out my journaling book, *Practicing Stoicism: A Daily Journal with Meditation Practices, Self-Reflections and Ancient Wisdom from Marcus Aurelius.* I highly recommend picking up a journal to help you apply the concepts you have learned into your daily life.

If you want to continue reading about Stoicism, please check out my other book, *Stoicism: How to Use Stoic Philosophy to Find Inner Peace and Happiness.* This book will provide you with even more tools and practices to assist you on your Stoic journey.

Also, be sure to check out my email list, where I am constantly adding tons of value. You will also receive my three-page cheat sheet for free that you can use for reference as you move forward on your Stoic path. You can sign up here: bouchardpublishing.com/stoicism

Lastly, please feel free to join my Facebook group, *Stoicism: The Good Life*, where you can connect with other like-minded Stoics. It would be great to see you there.

Kindest regards,
Jason Hemlock

Printed in Great Britain
by Amazon

40515065R00076